APPRAISAL AND TARGET SETTING: A HANDBOOK FOR TEACHER DEVELOPMENT

David Trethowan has been Headmaster of Warden Park School since 1973. He is a Cornishman and served for eight years in the Royal Navy before becoming a teacher. His degrees are from Exeter University and his teacher training from Birmingham University, but he says he learned more about staff motivation on a frigate than from any university course. Within seven years of leaving university he was Head of a comprehensive school.

David has wide experience of a management approach to schools, developed from long-standing contact with respected industrial and commercial companies. He now teaches part-time on industrial management courses and on headship training courses for a score of counties, educational institutes and universities nationally. He writes for the educational press, for the industrial society and various commercial publishers.

In 1983 he was seconded to Oxford to plan and lead the first One-Term Training Opportunity to train the trainers of headteachers. David has led, taught or been a trainer on over 100 courses for heads in all parts of Britain. He now runs his own courses in aspects of educational management including teacher appraisal at the Bolney Grange in Sussex.

APPRAISAL AND TARGET SETTING:
A HANDBOOK FOR TEACHER DEVELOPMENT

DAVID TRETHOWAN

First published 1987
by Harper & Row Ltd
London

This edition published by
Paul Chapman Publishing Ltd
144 Liverpool Road
London N1 1LA

British Library Cataloguing in Publication Data
Trethowan, David
Appraisal and target setting: a handbook for teacher development.
1. Teachers—Great Britain—Rating of
I. Title
371.1′44′0941 LB2838

ISBN 1 85396 043 8

Typeset by Katerprint Typesetting Services, Oxford
Printed and bound by Butler & Tanner Ltd, Frome and London

ABCDEFG 4321098

CONTENTS

INTRODUCTION

> Professionals have always resisted attempts to hold them accountable. It is the essence of being a professional — so the doctor, lawyer, engineer or priest has always argued — that one is not accountable to laymen and that qualification rather than performance is the ground of acceptance. This was so but today it is no longer tenable. . . . Society must demand that these people think through what they should be held accountable for and that they take responsibility for their contribution.
>
> Peter Drucker (1955)

APPRAISAL IN MANAGEMENT

There is no effective management without appraisal. Once a person accepts that management is working with and through others to achieve organizational goals, then appraisal is part of that process. It is not an optional extra. The person being managed is entitled to know what the organization goals are, what his or her role is, how successfully he or she contributed to the achievement of those goals last year and what he or she should do to make next year's contribution even better. Whether the organizational goals were decided by the customers, by the staff, by the owners or by society at large makes no difference to the need for appraisal. Why create such unnatural working units as firms, battalions and schools if it is not to achieve a purpose: why aim for a purpose without keeping those striving to achieve it informed of progress?

In schools, good heads, deputy heads and heads of department have always done this. They do it as naturally as they breathe. They do it informally every day as they meet a teacher they manage. Nowadays we call it feedback. They give feedback on what they themselves have been doing, on what they feel the managed teachers have been doing and on what others have passed on to them about the managed teachers' performance. Such feedback reinforces, redirects and recharges the drive towards the goals of the organization. At least once a year the teacher can expect to sit down for a much longer session with the person managing his or her performance and discuss in detail what has been achieved. To facilitate that discussion much of it will be self-appraisal by the teacher against tasks, targets and standards previously agreed. They will discuss not only achievements but areas for improvement and will prepare plans to help the teacher to develop towards that improvement. Maybe too in the course of that same discussion the appraiser will receive advice from the teacher on how the appraiser can solve his or her problems or improve performance. This form of appraisal benefits all concerned with it. It is constructive, supportive and developmental.

Unsystematic appraisal goes on now in every school and college in the land. Ask any headteacher, from primary, secondary or tertiary sectors, who are the least successful teachers in their establishment and that principal or head will be confident of nominating the leading candidates. Ask which teachers perform best in the establishment and one can expect an almost equally confident reply. Whether or not you are a headteacher, pause for a moment before reading any further and test this statement. Consider the staff in your organization and name for yourself teachers in those two categories. Consider next upon what evidence those judgements were made and whether those teachers so appraised by you are aware of your perception of their performance. This book is about open appraisals, based on shared information from which both the teacher and the school gain because the experience is seen by all as a learning situation.

It is clear that staff appraisal by those responsible for the performance of others exists in all organizations including schools and even in those schools which claim not to use the practice. The worst forms of staff appraisal are casual judgements, based upon knowledge gained by chance on random occasions and kept secret from those who have been appraised. Such judgements can not only distort development in the teacher's present school but, when included in a confidential reference, have a similar sinister effect upon promotion applications to other posts. How the best forms of staff appraisal are managed is the subject of this book.

Appraisal and target setting are the very essence of managing the school performance of teachers, because they are at the heart of all staff management in any organization. What does a teacher need to know to be able to give a good performance? The teacher needs to be aware of three things: responsibilities, standards and targets.

(a) Responsibilities: a clear understanding of what is required as the basic task, of what its principal accountabilities are, and to whom the teacher is accountable.

(b) Standards: a clear appreciation of what levels of performance are expected to be reached if the job is to be effectively done.
(c) Targets: targets are tasks mutually agreed between the teacher and the appraiser which the teacher accepts over and above the basic task.

Because responsibilities vary from school to school, task to task, class to class and pupil to pupil, even qualified, experienced teachers need to know what the school expects of them. The requirements to give a good teaching performance in Tooting may not be the same as those in Tunbridge Wells. This clearly understood task and appreciation of the standard needed are referred to in this book as the *basic task*. The basic task is defined as that level of teacher performance which will allow the school to function at a standard acceptable to those who carry responsibility for the school. The basic task is therefore at a high minimum performance level. Any teacher's performance which does not reach the breadth and the standard required by the basic task is a serious handicap to the school and as such merits time, energy and other resources to rectify the performance. The setting of this basic task is the subject of Chapter 1.

Knowing that a basic minimum acceptable standard has been reached may not be enough to motivate the teacher to extend beyond this standard. It is reasonable to assume that teachers need targets to stimulate further their own professional development. Why are targets assumed to be acceptable to teachers and to schools? The cardinal assumptions of target setting are that teachers will commit themselves more strongly to tasks which they helped to suggest and define, and that teachers like to belong to an effective department or school. Target setting is the subject of Chapter 2; the process is examined in depth and detail. Chapters 3 and 4 are devoted to the teacher appraisal process, whilst Chapters 5, 6, and 7 look at aspects of system design, introduction and appraisal training. The final chapters look at the special roles of the headteacher, the governors and the Local Education Authority (LEA) in relation to teacher appraisal. But before any of these important facets can be discussed, let us examine the process of target setting and its relationship with school policy.

TARGET SETTING AND THE POLICY OF THE SCHOOL

One reason society is so often dissatisfied with its schools is that it is not clear what it wants them to achieve. It makes little concerted attempt to clarify what it wants from schools, though individuals or groups within society frequently exert their own pressures. Industry, the universities and colleges, government departments, H.M. Inspectorate, governing bodies, the staff within schools, parent associations and the pupils, each group has its own view on what it expects from schools, but none has the power to do more than exert limited pressure or to remonstrate at schools' failure to meet its own particular objective. This is both the strength and weakness of the British system of state education, allowing it licence to be outstandingly good but calling heads insufficiently to account for the poor performance of their school. This topic is explored in greater depth in Chapter 8.

It is my firm belief that society has the right and the duty to make explicit through its elected bodies what it expects schools to achieve or at least to be clear to whom it has delegated this decision-making role. Nevertheless, in whatever way the purpose of the school is decided, whether from outside or from within, the head of a school has the task as leader to see to it that the mission of the organization is clarified. Any individual or departmental tasks set must be in accord with this mission. The mission may be expressed as policy statements of the school objectives. The primary objectives are specific results that the head believes the school should be achieving and they help the staff to be able to answer questions such as: What kind of school are we? How do we aim to teach children? What knowledge, skills and attitudes do we intend those who learn here to acquire? What is our policy on the development of staff?

An example of such a policy statement is given at the end of this chapter. The policy statement should be written and made available to all associated with the school: staff, pupils, parents, governors, local education officials. Based upon the policy of the school plans are made to cope with a changing future. Ensuring that the work of the school is planned is a primary function of headship; such planning implies not only a view of the mission of the school but the anticipation of future needs and the determining of action required to achieve the desired results. How are these plans accomplished?

The most common management technique within organizations for the achievement of objectives is management by objectives (MBO). MBO is a cascade system whereby objectives in a school are agreed by the head and deputies, the resulting departmental objectives are agreed by middle management such as heads of pastoral and academic departments and the personal objectives which follow from the department objectives are accepted by individual teachers. After a number of interim reviews all objectives are reviewed at the end of an academic year.

The appraisal and target-setting system is similar but without the excessive downward flow suggested by a cascade effect. Although as with MBO plans for the year are agreed for individual teachers, for departments and for the school, there is in the target-setting system a greater opportunity for those who wish to do so, to participate in running the school and in shaping their own careers within it. Any target that falls within the policy of the school may be suggested by an individual or department. One that falls outside the policy of the school, for example, a proposal to develop the skills for mixed ability teaching in a department when the school has stated its conviction that it is best fulfilling the intention of the 1944 Education Act by teaching in ability sets, would not be accepted. Targets might also not be taken up for reasons such as:

1. Targets which fall within school policy would be given an order of priority and might, for reasons of low priority against funds, not be pursued.
2. Targets even of relatively high priority which overloaded a department or individual teacher and so jeopardized the achievement of others might be delayed or rejected.

What target setting also does in common with MBO is to provide a management structure with a manageable span of control. Each post holder in the school manages about six colleagues. If he or she has slightly more staff in a larger department to manage then deputies should relieve the senior of some part of the workload to allow more effective staff management. The headteacher, for example, manages, agrees the targets and appraises only his or her immediate colleagues, possibly the deputies, a senior teacher and a bursar. The pastoral deputy manages the six heads of house or year; the academic deputy only the heads of faculty or department. The task of appraisal is shared by all middle and top management in school.

As head of a comprehensive school of some 80 staff I, for several years, conducted all staff appraisal interviews personally. The experience was overwhelmingly time consuming, inefficient and, worst of all, often ineffective. Targets were, for example, being agreed which sometimes ran counter to what the department required. Clearly, both target setting and appraisal are only possible in the context of individual situations and by those in close touch with standards, performances and needs. In a large organization the system has to be operated through the middle management of the school. However, my exercise in appraisal and target setting with all staff had at least one major spin-off benefit. It established beyond doubt my commitment to the process. Top management commitment to the school appraisal and target setting scheme is a vital ingredient to its successful operation.

THE BENEFITS OF TEACHER APPRAISAL

BENEFITS FOR THE TEACHER

Role clarification

The target-setting and appraisal system clarifies with and for the teacher what is expected from teacher performance. The first point of clarification made necessary by appraisal and target setting is who is directly responsible for the teacher's performance and for giving the teacher day-to-day support? In most secondary schools this manager or appraiser will be the teacher's departmental or faculty head; with the middle managers in turn being appraised by the head or deputy. In most primary schools all staff will probably be appraised by the headteacher directly.

Task clarification

The appraisal and target-setting system also requires that each teacher be given a clear job description in the basic task of teaching: a 'bottom line' accepted by both teacher and appraiser as the standard performance. Staff will give of their best only if they understand what is required of them and why. Falling below such a standard has to imply a review to discover the reasons, followed by remedial action, be it training, support, reprimand or other action. But achieving or exceeding this basic task standard must also be acknowledged and the teacher's contribution be reaffirmed through praise and recognition.

Participation in target setting

The main thrust of appraisal and target setting, this most effective form of appraisal of professionals, lies in the joint setting of targets, identified, monitored, and achieved by agreement between the teacher and the appraiser. The right to negotiate targets is not open to those teachers who are falling short in the basic task: automatically their targets must be the improvement of their performance in the basic teaching task. But for most teachers target setting is the opportunity to participate in department policy making. The system allows teachers not only to suggest targets for themselves but to influence the planning of the school and the department. Specific time is set aside to seek out the teacher's views on the goals of his or her own school and on the policies and progress towards them, thereby increasing the opportunity for professional communication between colleagues.

Another teacher benefit is the chance to discuss career prospects and to set a target which develops personal and professional skills. With such planning, a more purposeful direction for schools and more effective teaching can result.

Teachers are entitled to know that their tasks contribute to the department or group objective. The appraisal and target-setting system therefore not only sets out to ensure that the conflict and duplication resulting from unclear goals is minimized but helps to identify which tasks are most important to the achievement group objective and which are less so. Being part of an effective plan is a great motivator.

In short, every teacher has the right to ask of his or her appraiser: What are we trying to achieve in this unit of our organization? When I know what is expected of me here then I know that my contribution matters and I know that I matter. In the final analysis appraisal and target setting amounts to a respect for the individual and for his or her performance at school.

How did I do? Feedback between teacher and appraiser

How did I do? If the majority of teachers were to seek a reply at present to this question on their annual performance the honest reply from the school hierarchy would have to be: 'Sorry, but I don't really know. Not only was I not really paying "monitoring" attention to your contribution, but I have no means of evaluating good performance, though of course bad performance can sometimes be drawn to my attention by pupil, colleague or parental complaints.'

This 'no news is good news' approach is one of which all teachers are aware. Appraisal creates that special occasion when time is devoted to the teacher and his or her performance. Appraisal allows teachers to know how well they are doing, offering a fair and objective method of evaluating teacher performance. Even for those good leaders who go out of their way to thank their people and who look for daily opportunities to show their appreciation, appraisal is the occasion to show how much the teacher's contribution is valued. It is a means of giving credit for good performance; a chance to acknowledge achievements and enter into 'celebration' of a valued contribution to the school. It highlights problems, situations and conditions which prevent the achievement of targets so that these may be tackled rather than hidden. Such feedback and support tend to bring a sense of satisfaction and to encourage greater commitment. In this way appraisal presents an opportunity to remotivate a teacher.

Feedback is not all one way. Appraisal and target-setting meetings tell the appraiser how well he or she is supporting and developing the teacher. These meetings are also the occasion for agreeing self-monitoring practices with the teacher on his or her own performance. Agreed self-monitoring practices allow the teacher to get frequent feedback on certain aspects of performance between formal appraisal sessions without waiting for an appraiser.

Teacher stress

The reduction of stress amongst teachers can be a further important result of an appraisal programme.

People with few demands upon them become bored. Increasing demands at that stage are seen as a challenge and tend to increase motivation towards a peak of teaching performance. However, a continued increase in demands upon the teachers will lead to anxiety, poor concentration, fatigue and exhaustion. Much of the work of Dr Jack Dunham on teacher stress indicates that having someone responsible for a teacher's performance with whom that teacher can share problems and experiences and have regular, sometimes daily, 'moan sessions' will be of some help. But one major organizational strategy for stress reduction is regular feedback to teachers on their performance. Dr Dunham suggests that 'Each school should have a stress reduction programme in which a basic aim would be that the staff should feel valued by having recognition for the work they do by receiving positive feedback' (Dr Jack Dunham [1984] Teachers' targets for tension, *Safety Education*, Autumn).

References and institutional judgement

Not the least important implication of this approach is for the writing of references on staff. Reference writing becomes more objective, yet easier for the writer. Each teacher will know the tasks for which he or she should be given credit and how well these tasks have been performed. The teacher should be able to predict fairly accurately, even if not shown, what the reference contains.

Under target setting and appraisal one teacher's covertly formed personal opinion of another will no longer suffice as an assessment of performance. Targets and their performance criteria are known to the teacher and monitored by senior staff. Open management, with appraisals which the teacher is able not only to see and have monitored but to influence, is an appealing feature of target setting and appraisal. The institutional judgement is therefore less likely to be clouded by critical incidents or by idiosyncrasy.

BENEFITS FOR THE SCHOOL

Target setting and appraisal have implications for the organizational and professional development of the school.

Awareness and problem solving

An invaluable benefit bestowed by appraisal is institutional awareness. Those who manage others can get wind of the problems staff have through listening to them. The appraisal process makes the teacher's problem the appraiser's problem too and by being aware of it puts the appraiser in a better position to advise, assist and support. Awareness includes being sensitive to the working atmosphere and its variations. It may allow the appraiser to sense, for example, underlying conflict, which can be brought out into the open, analyzed and resolved. It will allow greater opportunity for management by consent, that is, consultation and the acceptance of reason by all parties being aware of the viewpoints of others. Such awareness makes the appraiser a better decision maker, mediator and manager.

Appraisal encourages an openness in problem solving with staff feeling free to signal their awareness of difficulties because they expect the problems to be dealt with. The judgement of people in all positions in the school hierarchy is respected with opportunity for its development in identifying and resolving problems. The risk of making mistakes in problem solving is accepted as a condition of growth, and the attidue of 'what can we learn from each mistake?' is encouraged.

Teamwork

Target setting and appraisal work through not only individuals but teams of staff, such as academic departments managed by the departmental head. The development of staff teamwork is encouraged, as are supportive relationships through the school staff. Many targets which staff accept will be contributions to the departmental or school objective. One teacher is asked to help another in the team with teaching problems, for example, Joan Brown needs help with the clear presentation of material to a mathematics class, or Henry Jones with the organization and planning of equipment for science lessons. As team members the staff may also identify gaps in team performance and fill them through the targets they set. Ann Trelawney prepares transparencies and worksheets much needed by the history department, whilst Phillip Biggs in preparing for promotion takes responsibility for stock control from the head of the English department. Areas of overlap and duplication too can be reduced to make the team more effective.

School ethos and the management of change

Through target-setting and appraisal meetings, people know what is important to the school and what is not, since target setting and appraisal ensure that the overall management strategy for a school is known and that staff have a common goal to work for. School norms are established and become explicit. In general, however, while it is based on a sense of order, target setting encourages the questioning of existing methods and swift adaptation of change. The management of change is facilitated through the same management process which exists for corrective action.

Developing a caring school

When our staff do well we need ample opportunity to say so, as do the best industrial firms. 'The systems in the excellent companies are not only designed to produce lots of winners; they are constructed to celebrate the winning once it occurs' (Peters and Waterman, 1982).

Appraisal is also an opportunity to show that the appraiser cares — not only about school-related problems but about his or her teachers. Exercising a caring concern means more than listening, even though that can be much appreciated; it means taking action to help in the teacher's development, career progress and personal problems. Caring schools take action to help their pupils, and exercise an active caring concern for staff as well.

School succession planning and handover information

A fifth aspect of school development is that of succession planning as staff identify career development targets. The school is too small a unit to undertake viable career planning and development for staff, but it can develop and provide experience for possible future posts elsewhere. In doing so the school provides succession 'cover' for its own key posts, even if it cannot guarantee promotion to those posts.

Target setting and appraisal provide useful handover information to a new headteacher or head of department on the targets of the team and its members. An analysis of the targets of a team of staff will reveal much to the incoming leader, not only about individuals and their maturity but about the team and its priorities.

VALUE FOR MONEY

Appraisal should also have appeal to those charged with securing an effective, efficient education service at reasonable cost such as elected members, LEAs and governors. Its attraction should lie in three main directions: the use of resources, the development of staff and the potential for control of education.

Use of resources

First, constantly appraising the targets of the school, its component units and its individual members of staff implies a continuing review of the use of resources. This review applies not only to finances, whether from LEA or private sources, and to buildings and grounds but to teacher time, effort and goodwill. If appropriate school targets have been set, then the most effective method of achieving them is through a system of appraisal.

Not only does appraisal encourage effective resource use, it also develops ways of measuring output so that we are aware of what is being achieved. Output measures in education as elsewhere are notoriously tricky, and there is a temptation for teachers to hide behind professional judgements which they are unwilling to justify to their employers and their customers. The Conservative Party booklet 'No Turning Back' asks: 'Why is it that education is so dominated by talk of inputs and parents are given so little opportunity to assess what comes out? It is because state education has become captured by the producers.' Appraisal, however, puts the professional on to the search for measurement criteria which are sufficiently objective for one professional judgement not to be used to block another and to allow laymen to assess success.

Maximizing teacher potential

A second attraction of teacher performance appraisal for those who provide an education service is that it opens the possibility of maximizing staff potential. It is not an automatic corollary of appraisal but it would be entirely feasible for an LEA to plan a staff-development policy supported by its school-appraisal system. Whilst potential identification should never become the major aim of the appraisal system, this spin off could encourage LEA placements of staff, in appropriate posts to maximize the effective use of scarce abilities and talents. Possibly this is what the Department of Education and Science (DES) has in mind as a major purpose of the introduction of performance appraisal.

> Regular and formal appraisal of the performance of all teachers is necessary if local education authorities are to have the reliable, comprehensive and up to date information necessary to facilitate effective professional support and development and to deploy teaching staff to the best advantage [DES, 1985a].

Exercised caringly, this active development policy would do much to build better relationships between the teacher and the employing authority.

Another aspect of the maximizing of staff potential is the effective use of training. Appraisal encourages more on-the-job training within school, reducing the LEA funding in off-site courses in those skills. More importantly, appraisal feedback allows the consumers and purchasers of courses, that is, the schools and the LEAs, to influence programmes of in-service training; it allows the training body to coordinate these expressed needs and produce effective programmes; and finally it allows feedback on training effectiveness. Courses initiated by the producers of training, which do not strike a training need and allow a dilettante approach from their teacher clientele are a drain on scarce training resources. The often quoted Rotary Club model of training (an address, questions, refreshment, farewells) could virtually disappear.

Effective control of schools

Last, appraisal and target setting systems in school must appeal to LEAs for the possibility they offer for control. Elected representatives and their civil servant agents have remarkably little success in influencing the targets, curriculum and performance levels in schools. What effect, for example, has the formal publication of school aims had since it became law under the 1980 Education Act? Appraisal offers the possibility that real targets could be set for schools and that schools would have the necessary organization to pass these on to teachers and to see them achieved. It is not an essential feature of the development of staff appraisal in Britain, but should the nation decide it would like to do more than mildly influence its schools, appraisal and target setting might be the way to achieve this.

COMMON OBJECTIONS TO TARGET SETTING AND APPRAISAL

IT TAKES TOO MUCH TIME

The most common set of objections to target setting and appraisal concern time. As we shall see in later chapters it takes time on the part of both teacher and appraiser to prepare for an appraisal interview. This may begin with completing a warm-up document to focus the mind on aspects of job performance. Each person appraised must know the purpose of the scheme and what is expected to be achieved at the interview. Even then, the interview cannot be rushed. It needs an introduction which sets the atmosphere and then a stage by stage review in a two-way discussion of performance, summarized throughout. The interview is concluded with the setting of targets and the identification of their appraisal criteria, all of which must be recorded on an appraisal document. Later there may be follow-up action, mid-year reviews, or adjustments to targets. All these features take time, which the inexperienced appraisee may see as a waste of teaching, marking or lesson-preparation time.

To overcome this objection both teacher and appraiser must feel that as a result of time invested, performance has improved, and probably that some of the additional spin-off benefits of the appraisal interview have been gained. Even if an LEA has allocated additional staff time to a school to conduct its appraisal interviews, staff will still need to be convinced by the quality of the result that time invested in this way is worthwhile. No-one should be too busy to step out of the engine room from time to time and take a view from the bridge.

Many heads are concerned as to where additional time can be found for their middle managers and themselves to operate the system. Let me make two points in reply. First, because the span of management control for appraisal and target setting is limited to about six people, it may well be that this system will be no more time consuming than the appraiser already spends in discussion with his or her staff. Staff management and development is time consuming whether done well or badly. In the latter case a greater proportion of time is spent on resolving misunderstandings, filling emergency gaps in the department programme, smoothing ruffled feathers after unnecessary duplication of effort and in correcting incorrect assumptions. Much of the need for these activities is removed by effective target setting and appraisal.

A second point concedes that maybe additional time has to be found, more likely to implement but possibly also to operate the new scheme. Would this crisis not be the opportunity to examine how one's time is spent? Ask yourself what your priorities are and invest most time in those activities which are high priority. Beware of activity traps: do you personally have to write a timetable, know all pupils, write certain reports, sign those documents, or is it sufficient to be sure that there is a system to ensure that these things are done? Think in terms of targets: set realistic ones for yourself and organize the time to achieve them. Think in terms of effectiveness, as well as efficiency. It will be difficult to contradict that you are at your most effective when the six people who report directly to you are motivated to work to achieve planned targets. Some of the greatest time wasters are:

Unclear aims and responsibilities
Ineffective and unnecessary meetings
Too much time spent on low priority items
Duplication of effort
Crisis management due to lack of planning
Disorganization
Communication breakdowns
Not having the time to do things properly the first time

How many of these would be removed or reduced by practising a target-setting and appraisal system? It is not difficult to argue that all of them would and that time would be gained rather than wasted.

WE ALREADY SEE EACH OTHER EVERY DAY

Day-to-day management is an important part of the staff target-setting and appraisal process. Ensuring that staff know what is required, correcting when this goes wrong and praising when things go right are the essence of day-to-day management. As the one-minute manager says, 'catch them doing something right' and give feedback.

Daily contact between members of the same working group in schools is remarkably little when compared with most industrial or commercial teams. Even assuming that every contact involved is a brief feedback on performance would invalidate neither the need for a long-term review of performance on a special occasion at least once in the year nor the need to plan individual and team targets for the year ahead. Daily social contact between teachers has an important personal and team-building role, but it does not replace performance appraisal and target setting.

IT'S A PAPERWORK EXERCISE

Paperwork, that is, the accurate recording of agreed targets, is certainly an important feature of an effective target-setting and appraisal system. But if appraisal has become a paperwork exercise and is nothing more than this, it is the most time-expensive paper exercise a school has ever devised. Why would it become so?

This criticism is saying in effect that the staff of a school no longer believes in its appraisal process. An appraisal process in essence means those who manage teachers saying to them: 'Let us discuss the things you did well and those you did badly last year. Let us consider together how we can ensure that the good things happen again and how we can remove the obstacles for those which went badly.' Any appraisal system which has degenerated into a paper exercise has lost its openness. An unhealthy organization fails to give feedback, does not tolerate mistakes, glosses over poor performances and sees personal needs and feelings as side issues. A healthy organization expects a joint regular critique of progress, learns from each mistake, confronts and seeks a joint resolution to poor performance and includes personal needs and human relationships in the range of problems it tackles. There is a great deal of on-the-job learning based on a willingness to give, seek and use feedback and advice. People see themselves as capable of significant personal development and growth. In schools which have lost their organizational health it is not at all surprising that staff say of appraisal and target setting: 'It's just a paperwork exercise.'

IT DEMOTIVATES STAFF IF NO PROMOTION IS POSSIBLE

This objection to appraisal results from a misconception of the purpose of the appraisal and target-setting process. Appraisal is necessarily a backward-looking practice; inevitably what is being appraised is last year's performance. The information gathered and processed in that exercise can be used in one of three main ways to:

(a) Predict potential for future promoted posts

(b) Determine rewards, that is, most usually to decide upon the salary grade for the forthcoming year

(c) Performance improvement

The functions of appraisal systems are examined more closely in Chapter 5, but argue that although any system can incorporate all three, one of them will be seen by those who operate it as the dominant feature and will determine attitudes and responses. For example, consider a system that asks the teacher 'Were any classes or pupils not satisfactorily handled this year?' The response to the appraiser in a scheme designed to determine who earns the merit additions to salary for outstanding performance is likely to be: 'Certainly not' — and *sotto voce*, 'If you don't know, there are no prizes for my telling you.'

Similarly, if the system's main aim is seen to be the selection of future school leaders, the reply to the earlier question is at worst likely to be: 'There was some unsatisfactory behaviour amongst pupils early in the year, but I adapted well, learned quickly and within a short time there were no problems at all. I'm now looking for a situation in which I can gain promotion and go on developing at the same time.' This may not be the teacher's true evaluation of the situation, but if the system is looking for those with potential, teachers will tend to hide poor performance. Only if the system has as its overwhelming aim the improvement of performance will staff be willing to answer honestly when help is needed. In such systems, staff are least likely to be demotivated by appraisal because it has set out not to select the promotable few but rather to improve the performance of all.

IT WON'T CHANGE ANYTHING

The appraisal meeting can become an irrelevant annual affair unless action is agreed and taken following the interview. Because appraisal is necessarily a backward-looking exercise, it needs the forward-looking dynamism of the target-setting process. The past cannot be changed; it can only be explained, debated, rationalized. The future can be influenced if staff personal and professional resolutions command support and follow up. One of the worst forms of appraisal is one which exposes to the teacher his or her own weaknesses and inadequacies, but does little or nothing to help to strengthen, support or develop the teacher in these vulnerable areas. Target setting and appraisal are nothing if not an advanced system of staff development.

IT WON'T BE FAIR

The fear of biased appraisal is a deep-seated fear that the teacher will be judged not on total performance but on a minority of isolated and unfavourable incidents, by an untrained and highly subjective appraiser. Our target-setting and appraisal system must be able to show teachers the task they are needed to perform and to explain how judgements will be made on their performance. Such an open appraisal tends to remove fears that it will be a 'nit-picking' exercise and also creates the platform from which the teacher as appraisee can begin to become involved. The appraisee's judgement on task performance can be more valuable than any, in an open appraisal, and by being so it reduces the teacher's fear of a subjective judgement from an appraiser which cannot be influenced by the one appraised.

The reservation about lack of interview and appraisal skills on part of the appraiser is a justified one held by not only teachers but their appraisers themselves. The Suffolk Education Department Study of Teacher Appraisal readily acknowledges this and proposes training of appraisers.

> Appraisers must have credibility and inspire the trust and confidence of the staff they appraise and to this end need to be trained in the skills and techniques of appraisal before the system is implemented [Suffolk Education Department, 1985].

The issue of training for target setting and appraisal is discussed in depth in Chapter 8.

There is little doubt that appraisal of teachers will become a feature of British education, by negotiation or law. It is a device which properly used can be the most powerful force for improvement ever introduced into schools, bringing benefits for the teacher, the school and for the relationship of education with society at large.

SAMPLE DOCUMENT

PRIMARY OBJECTIVES OF WARFIELD PARK SCHOOL

To meet the legal requirement of providing full-time education for pupils of the school aged 11–16 appropriate to their age, aptitude and ability.

The education consists broadly of developing and maximizing the potential of pupils for the good of themselves and the community by:

1. Creating and maintaining a suitable material, intellectual and moral, spiritual and emotional environment in which to achieve the objectives of the school.
2. Understanding each child and ensuring that he or she is exposed to, and enjoys, learning experiences and gains knowledge, skills and attitudes appropriate to his or her own development and the good of the community. The knowledge, skills and attitudes will include for all children:

Maximizing their formal academic qualifications

Preparation for family life, work and leisure

Development of self-respect and respect for others including their achievements, their welfare and their property

Developing experience in working in four main work situations: group work, individual work, supervised work and unsupervised work (e.g., homework)

Developing a mind attuned to initiating and accepting changes

3. Maintaining a good relationship and mutual understanding between the school, parents and the community
4. Selecting and developing for the pupils a staff of suitably trained and motivated teachers
5. Setting up suitable management and control systems to ensure the achievement of these aims

1 THE BASIC TASK

> A local authority, told that its bus drivers were 'speeding past queues of people with a smile and a wave of the hand', replied that 'it's impossible for drivers to keep to their timetables if they have to stop for passengers'.
>
> Quoted in D. Bernstein (1983)

All groups working together need to be clear in the purpose of their work, regardless of the nature of the group. This applies equally well to a fishing-boat crew, to the committee of Oxfam, to Marks & Spencer plc and to the smallest primary school in the land; all need to know their basic task.

The need for basic-task awareness is almost indisputable. Take, for example, the 'use of resources' argument. In a typical comprehensive school the community has invested the value of the land, the buildings, the equipment, the cost of heat, lighting and power, the salaries of professional staff and their ancillary workers. To what purpose? A school has an obligation to know what it is doing and where it is going. One who does not know what he or she is doing and how he or she will know when it is done has no business being on a school staff. A plan is essential. A plan allows us to monitor our performance, identify our priorities, assess whether we are on course to achieve our plan, assess the risks involved in change and make the appropriate adjustments to achieve that change. 'If you don't know where you're going you're likely to end up somewhere else,' as they say in Ireland. More seriously, how can we fail to accept the need for and the value of basic-task awareness?

We need to plan to be able to identify what is wrong and to indicate the degree of deviation. How else do we know where we are, where we are going or when we need to change? The process of describing and appraising the basic task assists with identification of purpose and of task control. As the head of a school do you know which teachers are making the most effective contribution to the achievement of the aims of the school? Do you expect to know which teachers are performing best in your school? How do you know? Do these teachers know how effective you believe them to be?

Should they know? How do the teachers who are performing ineffectively in the school come to improve?

Clearly at some stage someone has an obligation to let teachers know how they are performing towards the agreed objectives of the school. How can we help to develop people unless we know their deficiencies and training needs? One reason it is so difficult to establish that an incompetent teacher is incompetent is that we never established what he or she should be doing. Appraisal is a management process for not only task achievement but staff development and planned training.

LINE MANAGEMENT IN SCHOOLS

If we accept the need to identify the basic task, let us ask how it is to be done. Who, in your school controls what is to be achieved? Is it the head? a deputy? a collegiate approach? the caretaker? Next let us ask how that control is exercised. Is it accidental? exercised by chance? does the school move along like the *Marie Celeste*? If not, by what managed process are the basic tasks, objectives or aims of your school identified, agreed, delegated and achieved. Whose decision will it be, for example, in a primary school if a class teacher wished to reinstate ITA? the class teacher? the PTA? the head? Whose responsibility is it in a secondary school if, for example, the wrong set books are studied for an external examination? Is it the responsibility of the teacher who taught from the wrong books? Is it the head of that teacher's department? Or is it the headteacher of the school? Clearly the headteacher cannot be totally absolved of blame, and must at the very least accept the responsibility for ensuring that there exists an appropriate system for the identification of set books. It will, in most schools, be a responsibility clearly delegated to the head of department by the headteacher with whom control lies.

Packwood (1977) says of the hierarchical structure that

> Through a series of manager-subordinate relationships it explicitly locates the accountability for work. The manager in the hierarchy is responsible not only for his or her performance but also for the work of subordinates.

It is a prerequisite of target setting that each teacher has a specific colleague as 'manager' with whom to work. It is to this particular colleague that the teacher is directly accountable for his or her teaching performance and to whom the teacher turns for help, advice, support, encouragement, approval and appraisal. The appraiser's interest in the teacher's performance stems from being directly responsible for it, that is, ensuring that the teacher performs effectively and produces what the school requires becomes part of the task of the appraiser. The appraiser's interest in the teacher's contribution to the school is therefore not an altrustic one; it is an acknowledged responsibility, a principal accountability. It is not only a once-a-year task but a day-to-day role involving development, discussion and guidance.

How many staff in a school could an appraiser manage? In most schools such an appraiser will have a full, or practically full, teaching timetable and so his or her opportunity to devote time to the management development of colleagues is limited. On the other hand, an appraiser is dealing with professionally and academically qualified staff who will not normally need or appreciate minute-by-minute close supervision. In normal circumstances therefore the appraiser will be managing about seven people. Managing this number will be more difficult at times of organizational change or when the teachers have high expectation of development and training in a new task or when one or more of them is a probationary teacher. But in normal circumstances seven teachers is a reasonable number to manage.

In most schools the most likely post for the appraiser of teachers to hold is that of head of department. In small schools all teacher appraisal may be undertaken by the head or deputy head. The deciding criteria will normally be the number of staff in the organization. In a good-sized comprehensive school the basic line management used for appraisal might be:

Headteacher appraises	All deputy heads; senior teachers (5); bursar (1)
Academic deputy head appraises	All faculty heads (7)
Pastoral deputy head appraises	All pastoral heads (7)
Administrative deputy head appraises	All administrative caretaking and cleaning staff (7)
Bursar appraises	All secretarial and domestic staff (7)

Faculty heads would in their turn appraise their staff, subdividing and delegating the responsibility in the larger faculties. Work undertaken by any teacher outside the direct responsibility of the appraiser (e.g., outside the department or faculty) is normally appraised on a 'project' basis. For example, when a teacher has a tutorial responsibility or an extracurricular responsibility, this is carried out under the guidance of the person leading that particular activity, who gives performance feedback to the teacher whenever this is needed. A report on progress is passed to both the head of faculty and the teacher which they take into account at the appraisal and target-setting interview. There is nothing to prevent this report being preceded by a full feedback discussion with the teacher and the activity leader. It is not expected, for example, that the head of science department will be required to judge whether his staff are good tutors, run successful chess clubs or produce entertaining plays. But it is expected that the head of science will help his staff to plan their year ahead, advise them of commitments which will be required simultaneously, warn them of overloading and guide them to minimize stress. The head of department is, in short, expected to help his or her teachers to plan their year, to take on sufficient extra challenges both inside and outside the department to ensure appropriate personal and professional development, but not so many that the teacher's basic task cannot be performed effectively. This concept in line management of making each teacher accountable directly to one person only is important to not only appraisal but the reduction of personal stress, effective management and local school accountability. The organization of such line management systems in schools is discussed in more detail in Chapter 5.

There is no particular form of hierarchical organizational structure that is recommended more than any other for target setting and appraisal. The basic rules are:

- Every member of staff has a manager to whom he or she is accountable and who is responsible for the teacher's performance.
- There is no dual accountability. Teachers may work for more than one department but are managed and appraised by one person only.
- No appraiser manages more than seven people effectively.
- Every member of staff is aware of the basic task he or she is required to perform.
- There is a hierarchical organizational structure for the school in which levels of responsibility are clearly defined and a clear understanding exists of how each post relates to the whole.

ETHOS AND INDUCTION

Very few organizations give to their professional staff a job description which itemizes every activity and requirement of their work. However, most organizations provide a description of the significant, principal accountabilities of the task, leaving other aspects of the work to the job holder's professional judgement in the context of the organization ethos.

The ethos of an organization is its culture. All organizations have a culture which conveys their norms and traditions. Some organizations are 'thick walled' and tend, consciously or subconsciously to repel random ideas and changes from outside themselves. Much expected behaviour in such organizations is conveyed through ethos to support what is written as aims, objectives and rules. A Guards Officers' Club, a Welsh Valley Rugby Club or a University Senior Common Room maintain their traditions and practices mainly by careful induction (often through a mentor) and by consistently applied standards. Major companies such as Marks & Spencer, I.B.M. and American Express use the same techniques to perpetuate their culture — a carefully planned staff induction and consistent standards. Organizations which allow their new members to acquire the culture in a random and haphazard way and which are inconsistent in the standards they require will find appraisal more difficult because failures in performance will be more difficult to identify. Organizations which take these tasks seriously, however, find their accidental failure rate or 'mistake through ignorance' rate is lower and their rate of correction through colleagues is high. With fewer errors to identify, the organization can spend proportionately greater time in correcting them, probably to a greater effect. It has been argued that the ethos of a school is a complex creation.

> So this overall school climate which may be defined as the general atmosphere in the school arising from the quality of interaction between personalities, between various roles, authorities and resources within the school community; this pattern of on going relationships is vital to school effectiveness and involves all, pupils, teachers, parent, ancillary staff and the community at large [Murphy, 1984].

In organizations with a strong self-identity, errors and poor performances alike are a call to action to colleagues. People declare their difficulties and expect to be made aware of performance failures because they feel that these will be tackled as problems. People are optimistic that such problems can be solved, readily request the help of others and are willing to give in return. There is a great deal of on-the-job learning based on a willingness to give, seek and use feedback and advice. A collaborative appraisal of progress in this organizational climate becomes routine. On-going appraisal is not only accepted, it is expected. When, at the end of an appraisal period, the appraisee meets the appraiser for a formal appraisal interview there are 'no surprises' because errors and failures have been signalled, discussed and tackled throughout the year.

Such an organizational state should not be dismissed as Valhalla. Many good schools already operate in this way throughout all or in a major part of their organization. Their success is based not only upon good communication and a clear understanding of the purposes of the school but upon carefully planned and executed induction. An induction programme is necessary for any new member of a school's staff, not just those new to the teaching profession. It should aim to make the newcomer an effective member of the school as soon as possible by guidance on knowledge, skills and attitudes:

(a) Knowledge: of people, routines, and procedures
(b) Skills: professional, personal and interpersonal
(c) Attitudes: an understanding of the school culture and of the accepted relationships with staff, pupils, parents and others

Induction is one of the great neglected areas of management. At the very least, teacher induction should be a year-long programme, with planned units of content, a programme manager and a mentor, probably a head of department, for each new teacher. The head of department is the best placed person in the school to act as the teacher's personal manager and to assume responsibility for the continued professional and personal development of the newly appointed teacher. The mentor's role is to give day-to-day support and feedback as the teacher becomes increasingly aware of the kind of professional decision the organization expects him or her to make.

The period of induction is assurance to the school that the areas of operation not detailed in a job description will be tackled in a manner which the school can support and that if the teacher is in doubt there is an experienced colleague ready to advise.

HOW IS A BASIC-TASK DESCRIPTION CREATED FOR THE TEACHER?

However effective the ethos the basic task, which is a compilation of the principal accountabilities of the teacher, needs to be defined. It is necessary for new teachers, in case of dispute, and so that all teachers know what is required of them. Indicating job responsibilities and the standards to which they must be performed is an essential task of management. Every teacher's first professional target has to be to perform well this basic task. The right to set other targets within the school is earned only by achieving a level of performance in the basic task which is acceptable to the school. The appraiser's aim must be to ensure that when the teacher's performance falls short in achieving this basic task, the only targets set are those which aim to raise the teacher's standard of performance in the essential accountabilities.

The areas in which teachers are expected to produce an acceptable performance may vary in detail from school to school, but in general they will number between five and seven areas.

Some schools may approach the basic task by emphasizing the relationships of the school, for example:

1. Relationships with and management of children — within and outside the classroom

2. Personal relationships with adults — professional attitudes towards parents, staff, governing body, LEA, visitors, students, tutors, nonteaching staff
3. Knowledge of subject — ability to disseminate successfully, for example, at an appropriate level with adequate motivating of pupils
4. Classroom organization: planning and preparation, marking, display and presentation, record keeping
5. Personal and professional development — willingness to: attend course, share expertise, learn from other colleagues; development of personal interests; an attempt to keep abreast of current thinking
6. General contribution to the life of the school: use and development and care of resources, willingness to support and uphold agreed standards and policy, part played in the day-to-day running of the school, cooperation and adaptability
7. Attendance, punctuality and general level of commitment to school

Another school may analyze the basic task into areas of contribution to school life, for example:

1. Curriculum — planning, flexibility, standards/achievement, evaluation
2. Organization and management: planning, briefing, evaluating, organizing, motivating, controlling, disciplining, record keeping
3. Communication — interpersonal skills with: pupils, staff/colleagues parents, community, relationships
4. Commitment and contribution to ethos/corporate life of the school
5. Professional development: development of resources and support services, attendance at courses, development of personal potential, self-image and self-projection to children, parents, colleagues
6. Additional responsibilities

The preceding list is intended to apply to anyone in the school who teaches regardless of seniority, status or subject discipline. To such a list one would add details of any additional responsibilities, such as senior staff responsibilities, head of department, second in the department, head of house or year, deputy head of house or year, other specified responsibility.

The simplest agreed analysis of the basic task of a teacher may be one based upon the following 5-point plan. This can be amplified to produce detailed task requirements and responsibilities to meet the needs of widely differing schools:

1. Pastoral responsibilities
2. Teaching responsibilities
3. Personal skills development

4. Contribution to department and school community
5. Administration

Within each principal accountability will be detailed a number of specific accountabilities. For example, the principal accountability defined as *teaching responsibilities* may be further defined as the requirement to prepare lessons, manage and teach pupils, mark and evaluate the work of the pupils to the standards required by the school. This task would thus produce the five specific accountabilities: preparation of lessons, classroom management, marking and homework, reach agreed teaching standards, and academic results and evaluation.

In most schools what the organization requires under each of the specific accountabilities is not coordinated into one document which could be described as the teacher's basic task. Instead such duties appear scattered among job descriptions, in the school handbook, in guideline documents for tutors, in weekly staff notices or in the minutes of staff meetings. There is much to be gained for all teachers and for the school by coordinating these requirements into one document. Even though the role of the teacher varies from school to school, few of them present the school's peculiar perception of the basic task as a single entity. Yet one of the fundamental tasks of those who lead others is to identify the principal and the specific accountabilities of all posts. For some of the specific accountabilities it may be advisable to detail even further what is needed. What, for example, does the school expect by way of preparation for lessons? Teachers themselves will help to identify good practice and this can be included where detailed accountabilities are needed within the basic task.

An illustration of the detailed requirements and recommendations for a specific accountability is as follows:

PREPARATION OF LESSONS

Requirements

Resources needed are to be identified and requested from resources or reprographic centre at least one week in advance.

Programme/scheme are to be planned at least a term in advance and agreed with the head of department.

Lessons are adequately planned and documented in the record book so that another teacher could take over in the teacher's absence.

Materials prepared by the teacher are to be of high enough quality to add to department stock.

Subject matter must adequately fill the timetable periods.

Further recommendations

Define specific milestones and deadlines and document them in the record book.

Use the record book to help prepare in detail, prototype lessons, especially those which will be repeated.

Spend enough time researching the subject to cover the syllabus adequately as judged by ability to answer related questions from the class and the like.

Discuss your approach to preparation with your head of department or the like.

Any visual aids you make should be colourful, creative, imaginative, understandable, and so forth, and to a standard that you would like to be used by others.

Review your use of visual aids, worksheets and the like with the head of department.

In some schools such detail would be a matter of school policy, in others such specificity would be left to the department to decide within the policy of the school. The more specific one can be, the easier it is for the teacher to assess whether the task has been achieved. However, specific detail can have two major disadvantages.

First, it can leave the teacher with the feeling that there is no room for professional initiative. This is when the teacher and the appraiser may find it more effective to operate using the concept of the 'ethos of the school' discussed earlier. The teacher in such an instance is left to answer the question: Is the form of preparation I have undertaken for this class appropriate within the standards expected in this school? Decisions taken from this standpoint and in mutual trust must inevitably earn respect.

Second, too much depth of detail on the basic task can produce a bulky document which is difficult to use. It may therefore be best practice to produce a basic task summary which lists only the main areas of accountability. This summary may then be used as a checklist at appraisal times. Any detail collected to clarify the basic task further can be produced as a second phase document, used for reference when discussing the task or when initiating teachers. A copy of a basic-task checklist is produced at the end of this chapter. A copy of a second-phase document with its more detailed requirements, together with further recommendations under each accountability, is reproduced as Appendix I.

In general, however, laying out the basic task in detailed format encourages discussion between appraiser and teacher and opens the door to coaching by middle management of less experienced staff. Being specific it also reduces the scope for incorrect assumption. Many frustrations in an organization arise because a colleague assumed something to be the case. 'I thought that you meant . . .' is a discussion opener which frequently means that a teacher has undertaken a task unnecessarily or in a way which the school did not intend. The clearer we are on what is needed, the less is the likelihood of a frustratingly incorrect assumption.

A final important use for a detailed checklist can arise if appraisal ever goes sour. However hard one works at appraisal skills and whatever the benefits to the teacher and the school, there are inevitably a few appraisal situations which produce failure. Perhaps the teacher, even after support, advice and training from colleagues, lacks the skills to be effective in the classroom. Perhaps the teacher has lost all motivation and is not willing to produce a satisfactory teaching performance. Perhaps the teacher is failing for lack of support and wants to show the ways in which he or she is not being helped. Any of these cases could end at an Industrial Tribunal. Even there a detailed checklist of the basic tasks which the teacher is expected to perform will help to ensure that a fair and just decision is reached.

WRITING TASK DESCRIPTIONS

The first step in writing basic-task descriptions is to define the main accountability areas of the task. These can best be identified by asking: What are the principal areas in which this job must produce results to achieve its purpose? Or, in a more colloquial, and less positive fashion: Which are the areas where the most serious mistakes can be made? Testing the basic task against these questions will produce its principal accountability areas; the features of these are:

- They should, taken together, add up to the identification of the purpose of the task.
- They should not be time-bonded as targets are. Accountabilities are timeless and would be changed only if the fundamental nature of the task changed.
- They should aim to describe the end result of the task more than the activity required to produce the end result. For clarity these end results should be presented singly and not have several results combined into one statement.
- Accountabilities do not need to contain appraisal measures, since these may change with time. However, an example is given as Appendix II of a task description which includes some indications of appraisal measures, showing how these can be distinct from the accountabilities themselves. Where appraisal measures are shown, they can help the post holder with self-monitoring, a practice discussed in Chapter 3.

• They should be worded to emphasize the action required to produce that end result, and not be broad and vague statements. The action verbs most frequently used in writing task descriptions are:

accumulate
achieve
advise
analyze
appraise
approve
ascertain
assess
assign
assist
assure
authorize

budget

coach
complete
conduct
consult
contact
contribute
control
counsel

design
develop
dictate
direct
distribute

ensure
establish

evaluate
examine

follow-up
forecast
formulate
furnish

gather
give

help

implement
improve
inform
interview
inspect
issue

keep

lead
limit

maintain
mark
meet
motivate

operate

participate
perform
plan

prepare
present
process
produce
provide

receive
recommend
reject
report
represent
review

see
select
serve
service
specify
standardize
store
structure
study
submit
supply
supervise
survey

take
teach
train

verify

Four other features need to be added: appraisal, contacts, priorities and decision making.

Appraisal Each teacher should have recorded on his or her basic-task description the post title of the person who will appraise that performance. Also listed will be the post titles of any teachers who will be appraised by the post holder.

WARFIELD PARK SCHOOL

The Basic Task of a Teacher

Teacher: ______________________ Responsible to: ______________________

1. Pastoral: Develop and report on each child in the ways specified in the tutor handbook
   1.1 Know every child in the tutor group as an individual.
   1.2 Run the tutor group to create a personal and group relationship.
   1.3 Carry out all obligatory activities in the tutor programme.
   1.4 Identify and propose solutions to the problems of pupils.

2. Teaching: Prepare, manage, teach, mark and evaluate pupils work to the standards agreed
   2.1 Preparation of lessons
   2.2 Classroom management
   2.3 Marking and homework
   2.4 Reach agreed teaching standards
   2.5 Safety
   2.6 Academic results and evaluation

3. Personal Skills Development: Maintain programme of personal development in subject professional and managerial skills with the head of department
   3.1 Subject-related skills
   3.2 Professional skills development as teacher and tutor
   3.3 Development of others
   3.4 Deputizing and sharing responsibilities
   3.5 Motivation of pupils

4. Departmental and School Community: Contribute to the maintenance and improvement of an effective school and department in activities, attitude, appearance, conduct and in professional matters
   4.1 Participation in extracurricular activities
   4.2 Contribution to morale
   4.3 Professional attitude, appearance, conduct
   4.4 Contribution to effective department
   4.5 Contribution to effective house
   4.6 Attendance at and contribution to departmental and house meetings
   4.7 Contribution to department stock of teaching materials and to syllabus review

5. Administration: Maintain school records and reports and discuss with parents
   5.1 Department records
   5.2 Detentions
   5.3 School duties
   5.4 Reporting to parents on progress of pupils

6. Additional responsibilities
   6.1 Senior staff responsibility
   6.2 Head of department
   6.3 Head of house
   6.4 Second in department
   6.5 Deputy head of house
   6.6 Other special responsibility

Contacts Each teacher should be clear on who he or she is expected to contact outside the school. Does the tutor directly contact the educational welfare officer, social services, the police? Does the teacher invite outside speakers, initiate parent contact, consult the advisory service? Should approval be sought inside the school?

Priorities In some posts it is useful to indicate the chief areas of the job requiring initiative or giving scope to be creative or innovative. For example, although important, following the regulations of the various GCSE Boards is not intended to be a creative exercise. However, balancing and integrating the requests of heads of department prior to the construction of a timetable, may be the most innovative feature of a particular post.

Decision Making Another such feature is the scope which exists in the post for making decisions. It helps the post holder to know the kinds of decision which can be made with and without prior approval and also those decisions which must be referred to others for final resolution. Where decisions can be made, indicate the limits of power. Some examples are:

Budget limits, for example, responsible for school furniture and fittings with a budget of £3,000

Personal limits, for example, responsible for nonclerical ancillary staff and their recruitment

Policy limits, for example, responsible for academic policy with authority to create and change curriculum, pupil options and the like without higher approval

Where such priorities exist it may help the teacher and the appraiser to identify the key areas.

To summarize, the first target of every teacher is to achieve competence in the basic task. The first task of the appraiser is to make clear to the teacher what this basic task is, emphasizing its principal accountabilities and standards. As for the remainder of the teacher's task, much will be carried out within the culture or ethos of the school, but if this becomes unclear on any issue, then a more detailed description of that particular area will be needed.

2 TARGET SETTING

> When you are aspiring to the highest place, it is honorable to reach the second or even the third rank.
>
> Cicero

Target setting is not merely a management technique. It is a school management philosophy. It assumes:

- Teachers will commit themselves more strongly to targets which they helped to suggest, define and set.
- Teachers like an answer to the question 'How am I doing?' They like to measure their progress.
- Teachers like to feel they belong to an effective department, house and school. They like to feel they are making an important contribution to the unit in which they work.
- Teachers appreciate delegation and value mutual agreement on what has to be done.
- Once targets have been agreed, teachers do not expect to be told in detail how to do the job, but expect to use their professional skills.
- Teachers, like everyone else, work better when they feel they have some control over what happens to them.

Targets are goals which teachers are motivated to achieve. They can be professional targets such as the improved quality of work, better performance, achieving promotion or they can be personal targets such as self-development, earning praise and esteem, or the satisfaction of a sense of achievement. In this volume a *target* will be taken to cover terms such as aim, direction, purpose, objective, plan or goal. A target is, in short, something to be aimed at, something one intends to achieve over and above the teacher's basic task. Now let us examine closely the need for target setting for individual teachers.

Firstly, target setting ensures that the teacher's contribution over and above the basic task in the forthcoming year will fit effectively into the targets of the department and of the school. Teachers already accept the need for a syllabus, a school timetable, a study rota and other such plans to ensure coordinated staff activity. So, too, in other aspects of school life, teachers do not expect to find that their work is unnecessarily duplicated or that their effort is wasted because it does not fit into a plan.

Imagine the demotivated reaction of the teacher who prepared worksheets for her mixed ability group over the summer vacation only to find the policy for the new academic year changed to ability sets. Valuable teacher effort can also be wasted on activities which the school did not require at that particular time with that particular group, and no matter how worthwhile they appear in themselves, do not significantly contribute to what the department or year group or school is trying to achieve at that period. How many overworked teachers are taking on tasks which add a disproportionately small contribution to the success of the school? How many school tasks are undertaken by teachers without the knowledge of head of department, deputy head or head, who, given that knowledge, would not require or expect the teacher to undertake? How many teachers are unaware of what their own school or even department is trying to achieve, who, if the group target were made more clear to them would willingly contribute to its successful achievement? Contributing to a plan can in itself become a great motivator. Secondly, target setting allows the head justified management control. Let us consider a parable represented by the following diagram:

1980 A B C D E (F G)
1981 (A B) C D E F G
1982 (A) – C D E F G

Once in 1980 there was a head of house who in addition to his teaching (which we may call task A) accepted for his pastoral role four major tasks which could be identified as tasks B, C, D and E. He was keen to accept responsibility for two other tasks which interested him greatly, the clerical work for the School Combined Cadet Force unit (which we will call task F) and responsibility for all school fund accounts (task G). Tasks F and G were low priority because they could have been delegated to clerical staff and were only delegated to the head of house because of his interest and at his special request. The headmistress was delighted with the arrangement. By 1981, however, pressure of work in tasks F and G was lowering the house head's standard of performance in tasks A and B. This situation intensified in 1982 and by 1983 task A (teaching) was being badly prepared and marked, task B (knowing well the pupils and the parents of the house) was scarcely being done at all, but all other tasks, including tasks F and G were being performed well and taking all of the time the house head could reasonably be expected to devote to school-related work. He felt that he was a committed member of staff, performing well for the school, and was amazed to learn that the headmistress felt dissatisfied with his performance.

The moral of course, is that with an effective target-setting and appraisal system this situation could have been identified and corrected in 1981. The targets set for that house head would have redirected his effort into the two areas of tasks A and B where good performance was essential, and would have reduced the input to the level warranted in those areas which were optional extras so far as the school was concerned. Target setting in such cases allows the school to control the input of staff effort to areas which have been agreed as priorities, as well as keeping open the channels of communication on job performance. This is the target setter's answer to the teacher who wants to drift without supervision or control.

A third reason why individual teachers may need target setting is that they themselves represent a scarce resource. Teachers represent staff time, staff salaries and staff goodwill, all of which have to be used in the most effective way. Even goodwill is not in unlimited supply. Ask teachers at the end of a term to produce a play, plan a carol service, mark examination papers and run pupil discos and parties, and then see how much goodwill remains to meet and discuss reports with parents.

The fourth reason for personal target setting with each teacher arises from respect for the individual. The most soul-destroying employment is employment without aim and purpose. Every teacher ought to be able to say 'I know what we are trying to achieve in this school and I am happy to help. I know what is expected of me. I know that my contribution matters to the department and to the school and because of this, I know that I matter.' Every teacher has the right to target setting. This is the target setter's answer to the teacher who is suspicious of target setting and appraisal: a genuine concern on the part of the appraiser to help the teacher to remove obstacles to an improved performance.

A fifth reason for individual target setting is that it facilitates staff development. How many teachers should be undertaking personal or career development tasks but have not had the opportunity to be advised of the wisdom of these? Pressure of time or lack of professional advice has prevented many teachers from preparing for the next stage of their career. Target-setting sessions help to resolve these problems. Occasionally conflicts occur between the needs of the school and those of the individual teacher. These should be talked through at target-setting meetings. Few general guidelines can be given here. However, many a head has cause to be grateful to a teacher who was willing to take on a target to meet the needs of a school, especially in an area which did not appear to have particular career prospects. On the other hand, schools seldom get the best from teachers who continually feel that the school is thwarting their career development. The ideal target combines the needs of the individual and the school. For the teacher there is much confidence to be gained from knowing that a particular target not only provides him or her with professional development but is a vital contribution towards the successful achievement of a school objective.

Though initially some staff may feel threatened by setting targets, given a successful introduction, how much more valued, motivated and supported the teacher would feel if this participative device were regular practice in our schools.

TYPES OF TARGET

The basic task, defined earlier and concerned with maintaining certain responsibilities and standards, is every teacher's first target. It is an assumed but major target that this task will be maintained at the required level and that if it is not some school resources will be directed to help that teacher reach the level which allows the school to operate effectively. This concept of the basic task as a school imposed target has already been explored. What other types of target could be set with those who are competent in the basic task?

1. Personal and professional targets are those related to the individual teacher's professional development or the teacher's personal development in so far as it has a bearing on school performance.
2. Departmental targets are required to be achieved by a whole departmental or pastoral group.
3. Project targets are related to major temporary projects in school and may relate to innovation (devising new or improved devices, practices, ideas) or to solving a specific problem. They are interdepartmental or fall into areas not covered by departmental responsibility.
4. School targets are those to be achieved by the school staff as a whole.

PERSONAL AND PROFESSIONAL TARGETS

All teachers are asked to meet with their appraiser to negotiate personal and professional targets for the target setting period. The usual procedure is:

(a) Teacher prepares by reflecting on his or her own strengths, and weaknesses, talents, skills, achievements, likes and dislikes and on short or long-term career objectives. A staff-interview form or warm-up document may be used to encourage this self-analysis. (This form is discussed in detail in Chapter 6.)

(b) Both teacher and appraiser, prior to the target-setting meeting, consider and make notes on the teacher's performance. Two documents are provided to help with this, a list of last year's targets and a checklist summarizing the teacher's basic task.

(c) The teacher and appraiser meet for a personal private interview, using the completed documents to form the basis of the appraisal of the teacher's performance. This appraisal session is discussed in detail in Chapters 3 and 4.

(d) The teacher and appraiser next discuss the targets until they agree on their nature, number (not more than six) and format. In the meeting, when appraisal has been completed, each separately makes proposals for targets, bearing in mind not only the needs of the teacher but the targets of the department and the school. In case of a breakdown, the head of department's recommendations should be followed, but the recommendations need to be seen by the teacher as being feasible.

(e) Teacher and head of department agree on the support necessary to ensure that the target can be met and on how target attainment will be determined (i.e., performance criteria).

(f) The targets and the criteria are typed with a copy to the head, deputy head, head of department and teacher concerned.

(g) Progress towards targets is reviewed at dates published in the school target-setting calendar. Targets are set in July to come into operation in the following September. (See Figure 2 at the end of this chapter.) The first formal review is with the appraiser in the spring term. The final formal review is with the appraiser in the last month of the summer term. There is one other review offered to the teacher. This is a meeting with the appraiser's appraiser and is not only a safety valve for unfair appraisals or personality clashes but a reassurance to the head that the system is working as intended. Such meetings are often called *Grandfather* or *Leapfrog* interviews. In a small school, where the headteacher conducts the initial target-setting and appraisal interviews, the grandfather interview may be undertaken by an adviser, an LEA officer, or the like.

(h) These review meetings are supported by good day-to-day management, that is, daily contact and feedback from the appraiser to the teacher. The essence of good appraisal is that the review should hold no surprises, because day-to-day fine-tuning has guided the teacher towards an awareness of his or her performance.

DEPARTMENTAL AND PROJECT TARGETS

Each department (academic, pastoral or any team or a project team) selects about six major targets for the academic year, the usual target-setting period. In making this selection the department must see if it has a contribution to make to any of the school targets of the forthcoming year. If so, it may need to take that contribution as one of its departmental targets. For example, one of the school targets for the year ahead may be to 'ensure that gifted pupils receive an appropriate education' which will require each department to reexamine its procedure for identifying and extending gifted pupils. If the school is not satisfied with the achievements of the department in this respect or indeed if the department is not satisfied with its own achievement then, after discussion with the deputy head responsible for this aspect of school organization, it may form one of the department's targets for the forthcoming year.

Apart from targets derived from those of the school, other department targets are chiefly identified through a careful procedure. Initially, the department meets and its members propose targets for the forthcoming year, together with their priority. The meetings can be group discussions but must include at least one face-to-face private meeting between the teacher and the appraiser. It is often included in the meeting in which the teacher sets personal and professional targets with the head of department as appraiser.

Then, the departmental head discusses the proposed department targets with the appropriate deputy of the school, who agrees the targets (see Figure 3). In our diagram these 'deputy-level' staff would be the academic deputy, the pastoral deputy and the bursar. There may be some negotiation at this stage, since the deputy may want to challenge, to question, or to add targets, and he or she will certainly want a rigorous examination of the likely funding, time and performance criteria involved. Finally, the head-teacher sees and accepts responsibility for all target lists as being both reasonable and desirable.

SCHOOL TARGETS

School targets can be proposed from any level within the organization, and there are two main opportunities for staff to suggest these. One opportunity for each teacher to do this will be in the annual, personal, private meeting with the head that usually takes place in the autumn term. A second routine which ensures that every teacher has an opportunity to make a suggestion or to offer information towards a school target occurs when each head of department meets annually and individually with the department teachers to discuss what they would like to see the school or the department achieve in the forthcoming academic year or in the longer term.

Suggestions for departmental and personal targets will be dealt with in the manner already described but for those suggestions which relate to proposed school targets, the information is passed onwards to the appropriate deputy headteacher as the person responsible for compiling suggested school targets. A reasonable structure for many schools for this purpose is shown in Figure 1, but the structure for proposals for targets should flow naturally from the structure of the particular school.

Figure 1 Target setting — staff contribution to setting school targets

HEAD	*Head level* Gives final approval to school targets
Academic Deputy Pastoral Deputy Bursar	*Deputy level* Discuss, negotiate and agree on school targets with the headteacher
Academic Departments Pastoral Departments Service Departments	*Middle management level* Suggestions, and recommendations on school targets from teachers passed on by heads of department if gaining their support or made directly to the deputy head

The appropriate deputy head then meets with each head of department, if their suggestions for school targets need clarification or explanation. Each deputy head must eventually compile a list of proposed school targets, tempering those received with his or her own, and giving the targets an order of priority.

The final stage is for the head to meet with all the school deputies and, putting his or her own proposals into the discussion along with those which have been passed on through the school to the deputy heads, to select the top five or six targets which the school can support with money, time, equipment, goodwill, buildings and other resources in the year ahead. These targets will most probably become the responsibility of the appropriate deputy to meet. A typical list of such targets for one year drawn from many aspects of school life might be:

1. Strengthen links between parents and tutors.
2. Improve the appearance of the school grounds and internal corridors.
3. Raise the quality of the work of tutors in the pastoral care system.
4. Set up a computer induction course for all Year 1 pupils.
5. Ensure that gifted pupils receive an appropriate education.
6. Make effective the school internal communication system, especially in matters of routine administration.

Who accepts responsibility for carrying out these targets? In the simple model described here and illustrated in Figure 1 the possible final responsibility will be:

Target 1. Pastoral deputy, involving the whole pastoral care system

Target 2. The bursar through caretakers and groundsmen

Target 3. The pastoral deputy, possibly through in-service courses and on-the-job training

Target 4. The academic deputy, through a team of staff who may treat this as a project, or through delegation to a departmental head and a department

Target 5. The academic deputy working through all departmental heads and their departments

Target 6. Possibly a project for an aspiring deputy head, with a project team of colleagues

The head of a school carries ultimate responsibility for approving all personal targets set by teachers and team targets set by departments or houses or other groups in the school. The head also takes responsibility for approving the priority established in the list of targets.

Once the head has agreed, these major team targets should be communicated throughout the school. They should be repeated to staff at a staff meeting at the beginning of the academic year, and should feature prominently in the staff handbook or diary. Teachers are entitled to know not only what their department is setting out to do but what others are doing towards achieving a set of school targets.

It is clear that target setting combines formal opportunities for staff to participate personally in policy making in the school with a hierarchical structure for ensuring the execution of that policy.

WHAT ARE THE ELEMENTS IN SUCCESSFUL TARGET SETTING?

In this section we are concerned with setting unambiguous targets since ambiguity can be even more frustrating for the teacher and for the school than not setting targets at all. Targets should be specified by: definition, time, finance, quantity, feasibility, responsibility, performance criteria, and standards, willingness to revise, order of priorities, monitoring, and review.

TARGET DEFINITION

Objectives are sometimes set in an abstract form such as 'Improve overall performance as a teacher' or 'Mark properly'. The appraiser and the teacher may well both accept the need for achieving an objective of that nature. But do they both have the same understanding of what is intended to be done?

When appraisers agree to objectives which are vague, they tend to overlook the fact that their expectation through achievement may change as the work proceeds. This almost inevitably leads to arguments at the time of appraisal: the appraiser genuinely but mistakenly believes that his or her present views on what was achievable have changed little since the original discussion some months ago; the teacher, equally genuinely and equally mistakenly, views his or her actual achievements as being in line with the original intention. It is therefore important that targets are expressed as clearly, as precisely and as definitely as possible, and as end results, rather than processes or activities (e.g., produce 100 worksheets *not* work on 100 worksheets). However, although the overriding factor is to achieve precision in identifying what is being aimed at, heads sometimes detail and define every aspect of the method of achievement of the task to be performed, which can lead to loss of initiative on the part of the teacher. Too much precision in describing how it will be performed deprives the task of its element of challenge, the more so with mature and able teachers. If at review time this highly structured approach leads to a mediocre performance which the head does not like, there is a tendency to bring the whole process into disrepute.

Finally, the targets should be important to the achievement of the teacher's task. Trivial targets or those of no real consequence defeat the purpose of target setting.

TIME

Do not set targets which are never fully achievable or do not have a definite completion date. Avoid phrases such as 'as soon as possible' or 'at your earliest convenience'. It is much better to agree a specific completion and review date.

FINANCE

If a target has financial limitations, make this clear, together with the source of the funds and how they are to be made available and drawn. It can help the teacher to be clearer about the detail of the task to require him or her to submit an estimate of likely cost, on the basis of which an operating budget can be allocated.

QUANTITY

If quantities are involved state these clearly. Many teacher tasks are difficult to define precisely, so be sure not to miss any chance of an easily recognizable parameter such as quantity.

FEASIBILITY

There must be mutual agreement on the feasibility of the targets. Even so, ideally targets should stretch and develop the teacher. By selecting targets which follow established routines and do not encourage personal or professional improvement, an opportunity is being missed.

RESPONSIBILITY

Be certain there is no misunderstanding concerning who is responsible for the achievement of the target and of any contributing parts.

PERFORMANCE CRITERIA

The teacher is entitled to ask 'How will we know when I've done it?' that is, on which elements of the performance shall we make our judgement? In other words the appraiser and the teacher should agree on performance criteria. For example, one target for a modern languages teacher might be: 'To teach French successfully to Set 3D'. For this target the performance criteria might be agreed to be:

(a) The results of the French GOALS examination

(b) The number of pupils from 3D selecting French or French studies for their fourth-year course
(c) The view of the pupils as judged by the teacher

Few teachers would want to accept that achieving these criteria actually establishes beyond doubt that Set 3D were taught French successfully. Maybe pupils were 'crammed' for the GOALS examination. Maybe pupils chose French or French studies because they were deterred from taking other subjects in that option. Maybe the views of pupils and teacher were distorted away from an objective assessment of the success of the courses. However when the best criteria available do not provide the perfect criteria on which to judge performance, they may well in an atmosphere of trust between professionals be expected to produce feedback which gives the best evidence on which a professional judgement can be made.

PERFORMANCE STANDARDS

The appraiser and the teacher may then want to answer the question 'How shall we decide how well I have done it?' The simplest measures would be those which defined standards as *satisfactory* or *unsatisfactory*, but a better criteria rule is that the criteria should allow as much credit as possible for a better than satisfactory performance. For example, as a general guide identify the key activities under which the performance of the target will: fail, meet, exceed somewhat, exceed consistently, far exceed. These are not precise terms, but guides to professional judgements of a performance.

Some target performances lend themselves to more objective measures and may be quantifiable and measurable, for example, in a French GOALS examination a class pass-rate of 70% might be called good, whilst 90% would be outstanding, with 50% being disappointing and unsatisfactory.

Much of a teacher's work and many of the targets a teacher will undertake must necessarily be planned and controlled in terms of subjectives. Effective 'management by subjectives' requires:
(a) A definition of whose judgement counts
(b) A description of the judgement process and the criteria to be used
(c) A discussion of these subjectives to be sure the teacher understands them and is committed to accepting them

It is well to remind appraisers of targets that it is a performance, a task, a job which is being appraised and not a person and that when targets are being negotiated the appraiser is dealing with a teacher who is already performing the basic task satisfactorily.

WILLINGNESS TO REVISE

One clear manifestation of the trust necessary in target-setting situations is the willingness with which the head and the teacher can agree to revise their targets if conditions change. Personal conditions might change after a target has been set; a pregnancy, a marriage, or a house move might all make a target unattainable. So too might professional conditions change — an internal promotion, a change of responsibilities, attendance at a long-term course. Organizational factors within the school might also lead to a revision of targets — a revised option system, a change in curriculum, a restructuring of the pastoral care system. Keep an eye too on the current relevance of the targets, especially at times of changing emphasis on the targets of the school as a whole. Any target which is overtaken by events should be reviewed, together with its timing and its achievement criteria. Any change in targets, time-scale, priorities, performance criteria or measurement criteria must be documented.

ESTABLISHING THE ORDER OF PRIORITY AMONG TARGETS

Most experienced target setters believe that between four and six is the ideal number any teacher should be accepting at any one time. More than six can be a deterrent to achievement, less than four tends to place too much emphasis on a few aspects of job performance. Given six simultaneous tasks it is also important to distinguish their priority in importance. The 'time' criterion will have already indicated by when a target should be achieved, but if unforeseen factors mean one target has to be postponed or dropped, how is that to be decided? Indicating the priority of the target at the time of its acceptance as either 'critical/necessary/desirable' or in a simple numerical priority, helps to ensure that relatively less essential targets are not completed at the expense of those which are more important.

MONITORING TARGET PERFORMANCE

The appraiser should monitor the performance of the targets at suitably frequent intervals. How long these intervals should be varies with the nature of the target itself. A target concerned with department relationships can be monitored daily whilst a curriculum review project might be monitored at much longer intervals. Pass on feedback to the teacher as often as possible.

The second influence on the frequency of monitoring is the experience and maturity of the teacher in performing the task. Those whose target is to acquire new skills in report writing, in interviewing parents, in timetable construction and the like will need more frequent and detailed monitoring. So too will the poor performer, discussed in Chapter 4. Those teachers who can suggest for themselves targets which they have the knowledge, skills, ability and willingness to achieve, need far less frequent monitoring. Such monitoring of the mature teacher may be no more than an informal enquiry, 'Any problems with your target of producing a computerized assessment program ready for next September, John?' If we believe John to be able to set attainable goals, his confirmation that he is on schedule may be all that is needed until we reach a formal review date. He will not thank you for constantly looking over his shoulder and you can gain time which can be spent usefully with those who are less willing and less able than John.

Any monitoring which is necessary should be supported by interim reviews which will be a joint review by teacher and appraiser of targets, criteria and performance so far. Such regular feedback, with any agreed change in an aspect of the target being fully documented, means that there will be no surprises when the target is finally reviewed at the end of the year. If things are going wrong during the performance period, that is the time to advise, to coach and to train. Never delay giving feedback concerning the performance of a task to await a formal target review session. Never fall into the trap of allowing the fact that a formal appraisal is due next week stop the appraiser giving feedback today if that is necessary. If formal appraisal is used as an excuse for delaying day-to-day management, it is failing in its purpose. Not only will it break the 'no surprises' rule but the delay could exacerbate the problem.

THE REVIEW

The final point to clarify is when and how the review will take place. Appraisal is discussed in detail in Chapters 3 and 4, but every target should have its review dates, its reviewer and its method of review clarified at the target-setting session. As in all teacher and appraiser relationships the essentials are understanding, honesty and mutual trust.

A SUMMARY OF HOW TO FORM EFFECTIVE TARGETS

1. Express them as end results not as processes or activities.
2. Make them as definite as possible and avoid ambiguity.
3. Agree them to be achievable within a stated time period.

4. Make them practical and feasible, not theoretical and idealistic.
5. Select only those which are important and of real consequence to the job.
6. Make them precise, not too indefinite nor too complex.
7. Set a limit of one important target in each statement; avoid having several targets combined into one.
8. Aim to stretch the target holder, personally and professionally.
9. Allow opportunity for redefining targets if circumstances change.
10. Tailor the targets to suit the person, relating them to the teacher's career where possible.
11. Do not exceed six targets for a teacher; between four and six is ideal.
12. State the criteria for success.
13. Agree them to be realistic, noting underachievers (who set their targets too low) and overachievers (who are aiming too high).
14. Aim to make your staff realistic achievers, who set high but attainable targets.

WHO CHOOSES THE TARGETS?

Appraisers must recognize and respect a style of target setting appropriate to each individual. It is unlikely that the same style will work equally well with all teachers. The style adopted will vary with two chief factors: the willingness and the ability of the teacher concerned.

Teachers with both qualities will be enthusiastic and highly motivated when they can feel that they have set their own objectives. Such a person could be largely responsible for planning his or her own work and, in fact, may well be demotivated if the appraiser imposes a detailed plan — even if the imposed version were to be similar to the one the teacher would have prepared. With teachers of such maturity the appraiser should spend time agreeing upon a definition of the target, its purpose, time limit, the key result areas on which success will be judged and on ensuring that the target is one which the school needs.

For a teacher of this maturity, self-respect is an important factor. The teacher should feel responsible for his or her own work plan and for its achievement. The appraiser's main responsibility may well amount only to tempering the plan when it appears too demanding or over-optimistic. More often a set of targets proposed by an enthusiastic new teacher with limited experience will need to be reduced. Teachers sometimes take on far too many additional responsibilities or targets to be able to carry them out effectively. The experienced appraiser is able to assess the stress involved in a set of targets and to reduce the number of targets or alter their priority accordingly. In such cases, a participatory style is required; discussion and support are needed while targets are being prepared.

The five chief factors which should influence the staff being given freedom to set their own targets are that the teachers:

1. Want to be responsible for setting their targets
2. Are interested and can select important target areas
3. Identify with the aims and ethos of the school
4. Know how to set targets and how to deal with most problems which could arise from them
5. Have sufficient maturity to adjust targets when necessary

Appraisers who want their staff to set their own targets should help them to attain the five factors. Such staff development will take time. To expect teachers to set targets when they have been unused to doing so will produce badly designed work. For this reason the appraiser should consider what his or her teachers expect as a leadership style in target setting, and if effective target proposing is to be delegated to the staff then a training programme to develop not only skills but attitudes may be necessary.

At the other end of the spectrum of readiness for target setting is the teacher who is not competent in one or more of the basic tasks of teaching and has to accept a target for improvement, discussed in Chapter 1. For example, the teacher without effective class-management skills has to be helped to develop them. Target setting in these cases begins with helping the teacher to see that a problem exists. Then, by persuasion or by direction, targets must be set to develop these missing skills and so resolve the problem.

Skills-development targets are often the answer when a teacher lacks an ability but has the willingness to improve. When willingness is missing, the need for clearly set targets and their unambiguous appraisal becomes imperative. The teacher who has lost interest and wants to 'cruise' by setting easy or meaningless targets has to be told what is required. The teacher who is avoiding work, who is not marking pupils' work, is not keeping appropriate records, is not preparing lessons adequately has to be told what to do through target setting. If these targets are not reached and if the unwillingness remains, we have probably reached as low as we can reach in immaturity and unprofessionalism. In these extreme cases the head needs not a handbook on target setting but a legal guide to the dismissal procedure.

There are, however, some teachers who, although able in performing the basic task, do not wish to set any additional targets at present. In the short run appraisers should respect this and accept that, at least for the year in question, achieving the basic task is a sufficient achievement in itself. This is especially so when the teacher has personal adjustments to make, for example, a new baby, a death in the immediate family or the like.

Also, there are some teachers who prefer to have their targets suggested or even directly nominated for them. Team-minded teachers, for example, will often suggest that their targets be set for them so that they can be certain that these are coordinated with the needs of the department or

Figure 2 The target-setting year

Targets	Responsible for targets	June	July	Aug	Sept
School	Deputy heads			Targets agreed with head following appraisal interview	
Pastoral or departmental	Heads of department or of pastoral units		Targets agreed with appropriate deputy following appraisal interview		Leapfrog review meeting with head
Personal	Individual teachers	Targets agreed with head of department following appraisal interview			Leapfrog – review meeting with head-teacher or deputy head-teacher
Project	Project leaders	Targets set as the need arises, reviewed more frequently than any other type of target, e.g., Administration Computer project; Information Technology project; Introduction of GCSE, etc.			

If targets are identified first by teachers in June then by heads of sections in July and teachers. If the target-setting year begins with the headteacher identifying targets in by objectives (MOB) principles are operating and target-setting emphasis is at the top school. If the appraiser is to nominate targets it still remains important that the process of agreeing criteria is observed.

There is, therefore, no easy answer to 'Who chooses the targets?' Whoever sets them, the head has to be happy that the targets are coordinated with the general aims and ethos of the school and with the department and that they are set in the style most appropriate to each teacher's motivation and self-respect.

Oct	Nov	Dec	Jan	Feb	Mar	Apr	May
						Progress reviewed with head	
					Progress reviewed with appropriate deputy		
Leapfrog – review meeting with headteacher or deputy headteacher				Progress reviewed with head of department			

Targets set as the need arises, reviewed more frequently than any other type of target, e.g., Administration Computer project; Information Technology project; Introduction of GCSE, etc.

finally by deputy head and headteacher in August, then the target-setting emphasis is with June and cascading these to heads of section and to teachers in July, then the management of the organization.

3 APPRAISAL

> Judgement: The result an informed and qualified person obtains is supposedly going to be reached by any other qualified and informed person. Judgement presupposes information and expertise but is otherwise as objective as is measurement. We should be able to judge the performance of professionals and are perfectly capable of doing so
>
> Peter Drucker

WHY DO ORGANIZATIONS USE APPRAISAL?

Some organizations use appraisals to distribute rewards, some to assess potential and some to improve performance. Most organizations would say that these aims overlap and although they may do so, they should as objectives of an appraisal system be separated in practice, since the staff response, the technique, the procedures and the information required for each is markedly different.

Even objectives which appear to have only slight differences can affect the way an interview is handled. For example, consider the following appraisal objectives and their review emphasis.

Appraisal Objective	Probable Review Emphasis
1. Acknowledge the good work of a teacher	1. Favourable appraisal evidence selected
2. Warn a teacher that improvement is needed	2. Unfavourable appraisal evidence selected
3. Let a teacher know where he or she stands	3. Balanced view of performance formed from a wide range of evidence
4. Communicate areas for improvement	4. Areas selected for discussion will be those where improvement is most achieveable

PERFORMANCE APPRAISAL RELATED TO SALARY AND MERIT PAY

Salary or reward interviews are primarily for the allocation and distribution of pay, power, status and the perquisites of the organization. The reward will be based on last year's performance and will determine the salary level for the forthcoming year. Even so, organizations which allocate rewards in this way have to bear in mind that reward itself is not a motivator above a certain level of satisfaction. For example, some people stay in good schools and refuse promotion merely because their job satisfaction is greater there. For many people there is no continuous positive relationship between reward and performance. In fact, Maslow (1954) has a theory of the 'hierarchy of needs', from which Figure 5 has been adapted.

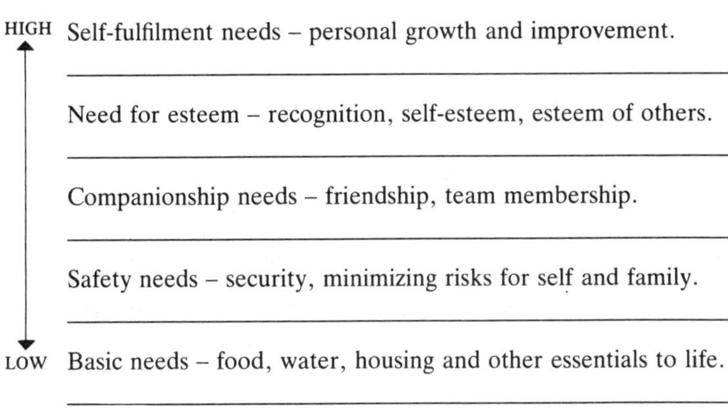

Figure 5 Levels of personal needs

In this range, the lower level, or basic, needs are satisfied first and it is only these which are directly related to salary. If teachers feel that they are receiving low salaries so that the needs which they believe to be basic are not being met, it will be extraordinarily difficult to use self-esteem, companionship or self-fulfilment as motivators. To ensure meeting basic needs a teacher might well forgo self-fulfilment or -esteem and take on part-time 'moonlighting' after school work is completed. 'Lower level' needs will have taken a higher priority. Until these basic needs are satisfied, higher level needs such as self-fulfilment and self-improvement will become secondary to most people.

Clearly teacher appraisals cannot solely or even mainly be used to allocate the financial rewards. The present pay structure makes that impossible, since the basic responsibility for the level of teacher salaries lies outside the school and with the LEA and professional associations. Only the scale-post addition is within the headteacher's power to recommend and even this does not require an annual review, since once it is awarded it, like an OBE, is seldom removed.

However, it is occasionally suggested that there should be some form of merit pay for teachers as an incentive, earned by a superior performance. Whether this practice will be introduced in Britain is difficult to predict. Sir David Hancock (1985) has taken the opportunity to confirm 'that it remains the department's view that a pay system which rewards exceptional performance in the classroom would be very much in the interests of the teaching profession and of the nation'. On the other hand the Suffolk Research Study funded by the DES reported against merit pay partly because teacher salaries were low and the criteria for assessing performance are largely undeveloped.

> Our visits to several United States Department of Defense Schools in Europe confirmed our disquiet about merit payments. Principals in these schools appeared to be unanimous in the view that the relatively modest payments they are obliged to make to a small percentage of their teachers for Sustained Superior Performance were divisive and caused considerable difficulties amongst their staff [Suffolk Education Department (1985) p. 9].

If this is implemented in Britain then the advice from companies which use a financial-incentive system is that it should not form part of a performance appraisal. Large merit additions tend to alienate more than motivate most staff since only a minority receive them. Small financial additions have little motivational effect unless accompanied by some public recognition of esteem. Even then, staff who fail to earn a merit addition this year for a performance they see as being as good as last year's performance feel aggrieved. On the other hand if the same teachers earn the merit pay each year, it has a demotivating effect upon colleagues who see the award as being too predictable. In many ways heads of schools are relieved of the task facing many industrial managers of establishing an effective reward-review procedure. Salaries are negotiated nationally and the only additions to salary, the Burnham Scale Points, are in almost every instance awarded to teachers who accept extra responsibility. Lack of flexibility if nothing else makes it difficult for a headteacher to use the scale-point system to reward good classroom teaching, since scale points are not returned and reawarded annually. The other three chief problems of the introduction of merit pay for teachers are: fixed percentages and quotas; lack of comparative criteria; and the effect upon public confidence.

FIXED PERCENTAGES AND QUOTAS

Each LEA will need to decide to what percentage of its teachers it can offer merit pay, with presumably a quota imposed on each school. Without a quota system, consider the financial risk of a high number of merit awards being made throughout the LEA. However, with a quota system, consider the possibility of demotivation through injustice in the level of award between schools. At the very least such a system would require what the Suffolk report calls 'substantial moderating'.

LACK OF CRITERIA FOR COMPARISON

To operate an effective merit-pay scheme that improves total staff performance and is not a disincentive to most, the award must be made in a way which is fair, acceptable to all staff and which uses undisputed criteria. Except at the extremes of performance there are no such methods to assess so finely one teacher's contribution, so that it can with certainty be rated against that of another teacher's whether in the same school or in another. Performance-appraisal techniques are examined in more detail later in this chapter, but by then it should be clear that effective performance appraisal requires the honest, trusting, self-critical participation of the appraisee. When salary is at stake, people are less likely to be self-critical yet without this the appraiser has few performance-appraisal tools with which to make fine points of comparison between teacher performances.

THE EFFECT UPON PUBLIC CONFIDENCE

Since only a minority of the staff of a school would be awarded a merit payment, most teachers, even though perfectly competent, would be seen as less effective by pupils and parents. At present because additions to staff salary are chiefly for extra responsibility, they do not indicate to the public which teachers the school regards as producing the best performances. Such a league of 'super' teachers could unjustly undermine public confidence in the remainder of the staff. Pressure to have children taught by the nominated 'best performing' teachers would be high. There might also be pressure on the school to select for merit award those teachers most popular with parents or those who gain best external examination results, in place of fairer criteria. This is not to argue however that there is no way in which additions to salary could be used in the interests of staff development. Even at present a few scale points can be used, awarded on a temporary basis, to allow, for example, a departmental head to delegate most of the department responsibilities to a colleague in the department for between one and two years, whilst undertaking a major school project, such as the introduction of Information Technology to the school curriculum or the computerization of school administration and records.

The experience can be a developmental one for the department head and the colleague, preparing both for their next promoted post. Such additional 'flexible finance' would only be used for major long-term projects, and should not be needed for most developmental delegated tasks.

To summarize, therefore, there is little scope for appraisal linked to annual salary within the teaching profession. The better policy appears to be to pay all teachers well and expect the head to devise the means to motivate the staff to produce good and improving performances.

POTENTIAL-RELATED APPRAISALS

Some appraisal systems are intended as their main function to be a means of predicting the kind of work the teacher will be able to do in the future and how long he or she will take to fulfil that potential. Could this 'potential-spotting' function of appraisal be used with teachers? To a limited extent, of course, it is already used. Many teachers acquire one or two promotions within the one school. Some may have been 'spotted' and groomed for a forthcoming school vacancy. But, by and large, although there may be some limited opportunity for promotion within a single school, the most likely body to be able to use potential appraisals are the LEAs. At present almost nothing is done to help teachers develop their careers, but given an operating unit of the size of most LEAs, then there would be scope to learn a lesson from industry and conduct a career-support system. With the increasing operation by LEAs of a 'ring-fence' policy by which internal candidates from its own schools are preferred to those from outside the LEA, the practice of appraising for potential may become increasingly attractive to the LEAs.

Dangers in the practice abound. Prediction itself is difficult enough, but consider related problems. What is the effect on a teacher of being selected, groomed and then not promoted because earlier potential has not materialized? What are the dangers of the 'self-fulfilling prophecy', which we see daily in operating with school pupils, on those selected for rapid promotion and more importantly on those not selected? In the light of this particular danger who should be informed of the result of a potential-based appraisal? Should it be only those selected, or should it be all staff? How wide a distribution should this potential appraisal have? The chief hazards in appraising to identify potential are: the recommender; training staff to identify potential; and changing types of skill.

WHO MAKES THE RECOMMENDATION?

Most teacher appraisal in schools is likely to be undertaken by heads of department and deputy headteachers. If we require these appraisers to make the initial recommendation we may be asking them to assess whether a teacher is likely to be able to hold down a job of which the appraiser has no personal experience. We might well be asking a head of English whether he or she believes a Scale 2 teacher in the department has the potential to lead a school, and to use as evidence little more than the teacher's ability in the classroom.

HOW DO WE TRAIN STAFF IN THE IDENTIFICATION OF POTENTIAL?

Since the practice of identification can have such a powerful influence on a teacher's career, the skills of identification should be passed on to appraisers. Yet it is singularly difficult to indicate what these skills are, let alone convey them to appraisers. On the other hand, selection by intuition is notoriously unreliable. Few people would be happy to have their potential decided by the 'hunch' of a departmental head any more than those in appraisal positions would be happy to make such judgements. However, many appraisers would be willing to make a contribution to the identification of potential based upon the teacher's present performance, especially if this contribution could be supported by other evidence from elsewhere.

If there were a set of ability or personality tests which identified potential and would be considered by teachers as fair, then training the appraisers would amount to little more than training to administer the tests. Such tests however need to be specially designed to identify specific factors essential to school promotion and leadership. No test at present claims to do this, and although several tests designed for industrial use claim to identify general-management potential they would need to be seen as reliable and fair by those who are to be assessed before they could form a useful part of the identification of potential process in schools.

CHANGING TYPES OF SKILL

The teacher who is mature, confident and competent as a teacher may well be unsuited to leading and managing other staff. Teachers who are able to comment intelligently on decisions taken by others may find it difficult to take decisions themselves. The dominant skills at the various levels within the school and within its external administration support system are not constant. Performing well at one level in the organization is no guarantee of an equally good performance in a promoted post. Equally true is that there can be teachers who are not outstanding in the teaching role but who could become outstanding administrators, advisers or headteachers. It may be impossible for them to be outstanding in their present role, even though they could be so in a promoted post.

Even if we accept that advisory, leadership, management and decision-making skills can be taught and improved, such a change in the relative importance of certain skills makes prediction difficult.

METHODS OF APPRAISING POTENTIAL

If potential is to be assessed, then a combination of three methods appears to be most promising of a positive result largely because the methods themselves are developmental and rely less upon subjective opinion based on present performance.

THE SCHOOL-PROJECT METHOD

It was argued earlier that if 'flexible' finance were to be given to schools that a more constructive use of the resource than merit pay was a project addition. Also, when discussing targets, it was demonstrated that a school has a need for work to be undertaken, not only within existing departments but on the project basis which may be interdepartmental or lie outside the work of departments altogether. This same notion of the school project is a sound method of giving opportunity for skills to flourish which cannot be exhibited in the existing situation. Examples of such projects are: computerization of an aspect of school administration or record keeping; timetable construction assistant; standing in as head of department whilst that post holder conducts a further project or is absent for a period of time; temporary appointment as teacher-adviser, house head, or the like; and preparing a five-year projection plan for some aspect of the development of the school.

Each project places the teacher in the situation which allows him or her to exhibit skills which may not be evident in their present work. It is probably the most realistic indication of potential and its duration can vary from a week to more than a year. If the target criteria are clearly set out at the beginning of the project then both teacher and appraiser will have a clearer conception not only of the success of the project but of how fulfilled the teacher felt in this form of work. This leads to another indication of the assessment of potential.

SELF-ASSESSMENT

Self-assessment alone is an unreliable method of appraisal for any purpose. Overestimates and underestimates are difficult to correct. In any case, at some stage the teacher in order to achieve promotion must be subjected to someone else's opinion of his or her potential. Few of us appointed ourselves to our present post. In forming a self-assessment some teachers may need confidence boosting, others have let ambition cloud their judgement. The appraisers task is to help them to form a realistic judgement, using the school-project method as a means of tempering self-appraisal.

TRAINING PROGRAMMES

A third method in our programme to assess potential can be training programmes which include simulated situations which the teacher might meet in the promoted post. Skill training and simulations would in this way be not only diagnostic but, more importantly, developmental. The programmes might include:

1. Leadership skills such as planning, briefing, controlling, evaluating, motivating and organizing
2. Decision-making skills
3. Interpersonal skills
4. Interview skills related to: appointments; grievances; discipline; appraisal; and negotiation

The techniques used should emphasize activity, structured experiences, role-play, simulation, and the like which give the trainee an active experience. This helps the teacher reappraise the self-assessment and gives trainers the opportunity to make their contribution to the assessment of potential. There should however be no 'secret' feedback from training courses. If the trainers feel it violates a trust and distorts performance of their trainees to report on individual performance then this should be respected and no individual reports should be sought.

Appraisal of potential therefore is not an easy matter partly because it may not be evident from current performance in the present post and partly because there are few techniques to help to form the assessment. However, taken together the best we can offer are self-assessment, training programmes and, most useful of all, school projects. When the school has made its appraisal of potential, it still has some difficulty in realizing that potential by promoting within its own organization. If the LEA supports internal promotion within its authority this information could be pooled centrally for use on promotion occasions in other schools. Otherwise the head will use the information as the basis of a reference when the teacher applies for promotion outside the present LEA. In general it is good for the morale of a school to see its best staff promoted whether inside or outside the school.

PERFORMANCE APPRAISAL TO IMPROVE PERFORMANCE

In earlier chapters the many benefits of an appraisal scheme were described, but it was established that in the teacher appraisal and target-setting scheme the primary end result and purpose is the development of individuals to achieve improved teacher performance. This improvement can be achieved in three main ways by: resolving situational problems; increasing motivation; and improving the teacher's ability.

RESOLVING SITUATIONAL PROBLEMS

Teacher performance is influenced by school organization, resources, technology and relationships with colleagues and with those who supervise.

The appraisal interview can be used to identify and if possible control these situational factors and to remove any obstacles to satisfactory or improved performance. The interview can also be the means whereby mismatches of teacher and job are identified.

Herzberg (1966) identifies many factors which cause dissatisfaction and most of these can be transposed from the industrial company to the school. Herzberg calls these 'hygiene factors' and says that they are answers to: 'What "dissatisfies" my staff?':

1. School policy
2. School image
3. Quality of my administration
4. Their relationship with me
5. My supervision of them
6. Other affecting relationships (e.g., pupil, parent, colleague relationships)
7. Status
8. Job security
9. Working conditions
10. Salary
11. Fringe benefits
12. Conditions of service (e.g., lunchtime duties, other supervisory duties)

The appraisal interview is an occasion to see what can be done to remove these as dissatisfiers of staff. Mind you, even if all these problems were removed, it would not guarantee a well-motivated staff, merely one which was not dissatisfied at school. Nevertheless, at any one time it is likely that only one or two of these are leading problems for a teacher. The appraiser's willingness to reduce the size of the teacher's problem will help to improve teacher performance. At the very least, showing that the appraiser cares will help to build an improved working relationship between the two colleagues.

INCREASING MOTIVATION

The appraisal process provides the opportunity for participation in target setting. This allows us to combine job needs and individual needs to provide increased job satisfaction. The appraisal occasion can also provide an opportunity to look at the longer term needs of the school and the long-term career plans of the teacher.

Herzberg (1966) identifies what he believes to be the most powerful motivators. Many fit easily into the school situation. They are answers to: 'What satisfies or motivates my staff?':

1. Achievements
2. Recognition given by me
3. The job itself
4. Responsibility delegated by me
5. Advancement
6. Personal growth
7. Cash, particularly when related to a specific achievement

Any appraisal therefore which advances one or more of these factors increases staff motivation and tends to improve performance.

IMPROVING THE TEACHER'S ABILITY

The appraisal process provides the opportunity for detecting gaps in the teacher's knowledge or skill and for agreeing a plan to fill them. The supervising proficiency needed to conduct a successful appraisal consists of communication, technical and human relations skills. What techniques are available to help in the appraisal process?

THE PROCESS OF APPRAISAL

In the Introduction I ask 'What does a teacher need to know to be able to give a good performance?' It is argued the requirements could be summarized as: a clear understanding of the job responsibilities (the *basic task*); a clear appreciation of the standards required; and an opportunity to set targets over and above the basic task.

Our appraisal techniques therefore must fit this pattern of teacher performance. Since a fuller survey of the available appraisal instruments follows in Chapter 6, here let us confine ourselves to techniques which best lend themselves to use with a target-setting and appraisal system.

The least contentious part of the appraisal process is that which arises from target setting. It is described in Chapter 2 how targets should be set so that their criteria for assessment are built into the definition of the target.

Targets should be defined as clearly as possible using any of the previously discussed criteria which may be relevant: time; finance; quantity; feasibility; responsibility; performance criteria; performance standards; priority between targets; and review dates.

The nature of the interview itself is discussed in Chapter 4, but it should be clear that most targets when carefully set allow the teacher to be self-monitoring and leave little room for discussion on whether or not a target was achieved.

For example, the target of having a new syllabus accepted by a GCSE Examination Board by September 1986 will speak for itself. So too will a target to produce a new syllabus for top Junior Mathematics by July 1986 or to achieve a 70% pass rate in a particular external examination. Targets which are agreed to be achieved are not difficult to appraise. The secret lies in carefully setting the criteria at the time of agreeing the target itself. If it was achieved, now is the time to thank and congratulate. Remember a target is something a teacher accepts over and above his or her basic task.

Nor is it very much more difficult to handle the appraisal of a target which it is clear has not been achieved — the syllabus which was rejected by the Examination Board, the mathematical syllabus which was not ready by its target date and the class which achieved only a 55% pass rate instead of the expected 70% — all leave us with three questions:

1. Why was the target missed?
2. What do we do now?
3. What can we learn from this target failure?

A discussion of the appraisal-interview techniques is in Chapter 4 but it is clear that in examining the first question we need to know what factors led to the missed target. Does the reason lie with the teacher, the appraiser or the circumstances?

The teacher

Did the teacher:

- Fail to anticipate that the Examination Board might reject the syllabus and leave too little time to amend and resubmit it?
- Plan badly, forgetting that the mathematics syllabus was a high priority item and was essential to complete on time?
- Fail to generate a good working relationship with the class and so allow standards of work prior to the examination to fall?

The appraiser

Did the appraiser:

• Allow a badly planned schedule which did not consider the possibility of an initial rejection of the syllabus by the Examination Board?

• Expect the teacher to be involved in too many other school activities just at the time when he or she expected to do most work on the mathematics syllabus?

• Misjudge the ability of the class when encouraging the teacher to set a target pass-rate of 70% instead of adhering to the original suggestion of 50%?

The circumstances

Were there unforeseen circumstances which prevented the achievement of the target? For example,

• Did the GCSE Board not publish its criteria for the acceptance of a Mode 3 syllabus until it was too late to change the school submission?

• Were colleagues unexpectedly ill for long periods, requiring much extra work from the teacher to cover their commitments?

• Did industrial action by a large proportion of the staff mean that this class lost many lessons during its final year of preparation, resulting in lower grades than expected for some pupils?

Whatever the cause, conduct the review without rancour, in a constructive atmosphere of trust. The aim is that teacher and appraiser shall contribute openly and honestly their perception of why the target was missed. Which teacher is likely to do this unless it is obvious that all the appraiser seeks is an improved performance? Be assured that if next year's salary or removal from a 'superstars' promotion list is at stake the teacher will be tempted to defend his or her action to the end.

Having agreed why the target was missed we now decide how to take corrective action.

(a) Can we resubmit our syllabus with the help of others in the department so that we are behind our schedule as little as possible?

(b) Is the teacher willing to work on this syllabus during the early part of the summer vacation so that we may still have our top Juniors Mathematics syllabus ready for use in September?

(c) Can we look again at the results of individual pupils we had expected to pass that external examination and see if they can be encouraged to resit in November?

The target-setting and appraisal system will not allow us to let the teacher stew in his or her own juice. In the healthy school when there is a crisis, as in these cases, people work together until the crisis is over; there is a sharing of responsibility to save the situation.

With the salvage action agreed the teacher and appraiser now ask the last of the three questions, What can we learn from this target failure? What can be learned depends on what went wrong, but let us suppose that in each case the target was missed because of a failure on the part of the teacher. In each of the instances examined the teacher who failed did so from lack of knowledge — of the procedures of an Examination Board — lack of skill — in adhering to priorities of personal time management when accepting a critical target — and, in the last instance, lack of teaching skill — to motivate a class of pupils. In all these cases the teachers need tuition, help and advice to improve their performance in future. If a reprimand is needed, now is the time to deliver it — when the teacher can see that he or she has been helped to minimize the effects of a missed target and is being given training and support for the future. If 'unforeseen circumstances' caused these targets to be missed there is little we can do but ensure that these circumtances are not 'unforeseen' next time they happen.

Finally, if the appraiser is to blame then he or she too has to be not only humble enough to admit it and apologize but sufficiently professional to identify and acquire the missing knowledge or skills. An appraisal scheme appraises *both* teacher and appraiser.

The most difficult target appraisals to handle are those when the teacher and the appraiser cannot agree. If the disagreement is over whether the target has been achieved, then the lesson to learn is that time spent in identifying the criteria for successful performance is time well spent. If the disagreement is over where the reason for the target failure lies then in all cases the appraiser should take seriously what the teacher believes to be the cause. Trust and cooperate with the teacher until it is clear that the teacher cannot be trusted and cooperative.

It may be that with a somewhat immature or insecure teacher he or she needs to apportion most of the blame elsewhere before conceding that some of it lies with the target holder. Only at this stage, when the teacher personally believes that he or she has a problem to be solved will he or she be willing to work to resolve it. While teachers believe that the problem lies only with the appraiser or elsewhere and not with themselves, there will be no genuine action on their part to learn from the situation. There is, of course, the possibility that you, the appraiser, are the entire cause of the missed target. The teacher, much as it may be difficult to admit, may be correct in the distribution of blame.

APPRAISING THE BASIC TASK

Let us now turn to the part of the work of a teacher called the basic task. This is defined as that level of teacher performance which will allow the school to function at a standard acceptable to those who carry responsibility for the school. It requires the school to identify the teacher's main responsibilities and to convey the acceptable standards of performance. How are these to be appraised? How are gaps in the teacher's knowledge and skill in the basic task area to be detected, so that a plan may be agreed to fill them?

The most effective and acceptable appraisal practices for appraising performance in the basic task of teachers are three: appraisal on collated feedback; support checklist appraisal; and self-monitoring and self-appraisal.

APPRAISAL ON COLLATED FEEDBACK

Teaching unlike a manufacturing process cannot be monitored at every stage. It is not feasible to watch a teacher in action all the time. Although in some parts of the performance fair and reasonable targets can be imposed from outside the classroom, other parts of the role require the teacher personally to identify what can be achieved with a class and then to set out to choose the method and to achieve it. It is therefore the exceptions in a performance which most easily gain the attention of an appraiser. It is the areas highlighted by exceptional performance which are much more likely to attract feedback. Exceptions may be performance superlatives, outstandingly good results, brilliant lessons, valued contributions and the like, which when they occur and at appraisal time will earn approval. However, the exceptions might equally well be performance failures — ill-disciplined lessons, poor departmental or personal organization, friction between colleagues.

Appraising the performance of professionals such as teachers does depend largely on the appraiser being alert to signals of exceptions in a teacher's performance. Almost any overt method of finding out what is going on in an organization can be used if it is with the knowledge of the teacher. These methods broadly consist of: feedback from consumers (parents, pupils, employers); feedback from colleagues (teachers, ancillary staff, governors, inspectors); and management by walking about (MBWA).

Feedback from consumers

Who are the consumers of education? The pupils, their parents and their employers can provide consumer feedback on a school, its departments, the effectiveness of its staff and the relevance of its curriculum. No school should run a 'snitch' system of collected gossip about the school and its staff, but there are recognized professional methods of collecting information. The method and the resulting information should always be available to both the teacher and the appraiser. Information gathering methods include practices such as interviewing, even when that interview was set up for another purpose.

Take advantage of the many personal private interviews the appraiser holds with pupils, parents or employers to explore ways in which the school or department can be more effective. The interviews may expose positive and negative views about many aspects of the school, for example, the effectiveness of a teaching or managerial style, the lack of clarity of aims, misunderstandings about purposes and attitudes. Encourage comment by questions such as: What do you feel we do well at this school? What could be done more effectively? Do you feel you are kept in touch with what goes on? What can we do to expose and resolve problems? Do you have any advice to offer to help staff do their job better? A further method of obtaining pupil feedback is to use the Image Comparison Exercise (ICE) devised by Barry West at the Counselling and Career Development Unit, Leeds University, in 1986. This allows pupil feedback to be processed confidentially by microcomputer.

The disadvantages of this practice are that interviewing takes both time and skill. Time the appraiser will find if he or she rates the research as sufficiently important. Skill takes practice if it is to encourage others to offer ideas and to share a trust. On the interviewer's part the most natural danger is a tendency to close up, reject the information and verbally attack the very consumer who can offer the most incisive and telling perspective on school and staff performance. Share, including verbatim quotes if appropriate, any information gathered with the teacher concerned, so that appraiser and teacher together may discuss how it is to be used, if indeed they decide to use it at all.

Unsolicited consumer feedback will continue to contribute through: the letters and verbal comments of parents, the option choices of the pupils, pupil reaction and similar sources. To these may be added surveys and questionnaires to any consumer group or subgroup. Consumer satisfaction is a major criterion of an effective school; listening to them, thinking like them, anticipating their needs and solving their problems are all ways of collecting feedback on how schools, departments and teachers are performing.

Feedback from colleagues

Another perspective on how well the school is performing can be supplied by colleagues. Departmental discussions, or if the school is small enough a whole staff discussion, give the teacher and the appraiser a further professional insight into how individuals and staff teams are performing.

A personal interview with a teacher can also provide professional feedback on colleagues. The warm-up document discussed in Chapter 7 often includes a question such as: Has any one in particular on the staff been of special help this year? Replies to this can tell not only what kind of help was needed but who found the time and expertise to provide it. Interviews can be supplemented with questionnaires to collect information as part of a planned strategy for keeping teachers informed of how their performance is seen by others and of jointly planning any proposed change in that performance. Such devices are widely accepted and are valuable for self-confrontation, for learning and as stepping stones to interpersonal confrontations.

Finally, the term *colleagues* can be defined more widely than merely colleagues in the same department. Useful feedback could come from any teacher in the school, from the ancillary staff or possibly a member of the governing body. The appraiser should also be receptive to feedback from those colleagues who are at the school less regularly, but have a wider purview for comparison. Such professional visitors include advisers, inspectors and colleagues from other schools.

Once again there should be the same open sharing of information between teachers and appraiser. Any attempt by the appraiser to conceal feedback which has been received or to act upon it without the teacher's knowledge will damage the trust which is essential to the appraisal process. The greatest dangers in management through exception are:

- Noticing only the crises and disasters. This can result in a state similar to fire fighting when it is too late to tackle the cause and there is only time to tackle the crisis it has created.
- Being sufficiently receptive to detect only major or repeated exceptions thus allowing some poor performance items to pass as acceptable.
- Concentrating too heavily on the exception alone, and so failing to give positive feedback to the teacher on the good but unexceptional performance.

Nevertheless, the aim in a healthy organization has to be to confront all poor performances and seek a joint resolution. A poor performance is a shared responsibility between teacher and appraiser.

Management by walking about (MBWA)

A parody of management by objectives (MBO), management by walking about (MBWA) embodies an age-old leadership and management practice. Walking the job keeps the appraiser in personal touch with how the organization is working, day to day. In schools where senior staff offer support and advice for junior colleagues they seldom find their presence resented in lessons or in any other potential crisis situations which teachers are expected to control. First-hand knowledge, shared by teacher and appraiser, provides an excellent common basis for the appraisal interview discussion. *A Passion for Excellence* (Peters and Austin, 1985) is full of examples of those who manage others being most accurately in touch with performance by being close to it. The practice of MBWA when transposed into schools means not only headteachers and senior staff walking the school at times of maximum pupil movement but teachers expecting to have their senior colleague appraisers visiting lessons at any time to witness staff and pupil performance at first hand. Much more can be learned about the effectiveness of a teacher by making eighteen unexpected five-minute visits to lessons than by watching one carefully prepared shop-window lesson lasting an hour and a half. I am referring not to the much despised practice of a departmental head pretending to be looking for a book in order to visit the lesson of a colleague but rather to a professional awareness on the part of appraiser and teacher that there will be visits to lessons as of right for staying in touch with the teacher's performance. One benefit I have seen growing from a greater acceptance of colleague visits is the more accurate detection and earlier discussion of the technique problems of a teacher. No longer is it necessary to await a parental protest, a classroom incident or disastrous results to initiate discussion on teacher performance problems. MBWA leads to regular open discussion of problems as well as does support in the resolution becoming routine practice.

Feedback vs appraisal

Appraisal may be defined as feedback with responsibility. That is, one person who is responsible for the performance of another evaluating last year's contribution by the colleague and seeking to improve next year's. There are, of course, other sources of feedback, since there are many viewpoints. A teacher's performance may be seen from the viewpoint of the teacher himself or herself, pupils, parents, colleagues and many others who are in some way affected by it. We have already noted that the good appraiser tries to include as much as possible appropriate feedback from these other sources in forming his or her appraisal, because it is upon this combined view, which the appraiser is responsible for providing, that action through the organization will be taken. The view of the teacher's performance agreed in the appraisal interview is the one which takes priority in earning school resources to bring about a change next year. This is not to invalidate the feedback on a teacher's performance from other sources.

Some sources are particularly well informed on aspects of a teacher's effective contribution to a school. Parents may be as aware as anyone what homework is set for children; pupils may be better informed than anyone on how effective a teacher is in the classroom, colleagues may be aware more than anyone else of a lack of contribution to making the department effective. But in the final analysis these are only forms of feedback. None of these groups is responsible for managing the teacher's performance; so the teacher unwilling or unable to accept the feedback received from these sources may continue failing to act upon it. When, however, the feedback becomes feedback with responsibility from an appraiser charged with the responsibility of managing that teacher's performance, the teacher is not in a position to ignore it. The appraiser saying to the teacher 'From all the feedback you and I have at our disposal, such as pupil reaction, lesson observation, parental comment, colleagues' advice and your own rationalization of the situation, it is clear that you have been insufficiently well prepared when you taught 5.1A mathematics over the past two months' is also saying 'And I have the responsibility of making sure that you are better prepared in future.' There is also the danger that the sensitive teacher may react to all feedback when some is best ignored. Even the mature, well-balanced, capable teacher needs to know which feedback the school expects him or her to act upon and which to leave. Trying to react to too many feedback sources, much of it conflicting, is a major source of stress for the teachers. The teacher is entitled to know, from the appraiser who is responsible for the teacher's performance, which form of feedback is going to be accepted and acted upon and to what extent. Whatever style is used to bring about the improvement clearly feedback with responsibility is the only form on which the teacher is required to act or accept the consequences. This is the feedback from the person appointed to appraise his or her performance.

In general, these methods require the appraiser to be open to receive feedback from almost any source. This does not mean the appraiser must act upon all that is received. Such feedback needs to be not only checked for veracity but sifted through the colander of commonsense and maturity. However, being willing to look and listen is essential to any method of effecting staff appraisal.

After a performance failure is detected, what happens next? Do we await the next appraisal occasion? It is important that awareness and improvement begin immediately. A daily plan to follow is one based on the one-minute manager:

1. Be sure that all teachers understand what their basic tasks and targets are. Clarify any misunderstandings and agree what you expect them to do.
2. Explain that the person in the school who is the appraiser will give regular and frequent feedback on how well he or she is doing.
3. If teachers are performing well, the appraiser will tell them immediately, saying exactly what they did that was so good and how it helps towards the school aims and targets. The appraiser's task in that situation is to thank them and make them feel pleased that their work is appreciated by someone who understands it and is affected by it.
4. If a teacher does something badly, the appraiser's task remains the same, that is, to tell the teacher exactly what was wrong and present the facts as the appraiser sees them, being descriptive not evaluative. Then let the teacher explain the facts as he or she sees them. Appropriately and privately reprimand the teacher if this is necessary. Be sure that the teacher is clear that it is only this incident that earned the reprimand, not he or she as a person and not his or her total performance. Realize that when a reprimand is over it is *over*.

With this system of day-to-day appraisal there can be no surprises when we come to the formal appraisal interview.

SUPPORT CHECKLIST APPRAISAL

One method of overcoming the last disadvantages of management by exception is the support checklist. An example of such a checklist is included as Appendix I at the end of the book, although clearly this checklist will vary with the school. A further example of a support checklist may be found in the Suffolk Education Department Study (1985, p 99). Neither list is meant to be either exhaustive or prescriptive.

The support checklist is an example of a directed appraisal. Open appraisal begins with a blank sheet and allows the teacher and the appraiser to decide what to assess. This has the advantage of encouraging dialogue and participation, allowing variety, and removes the danger of appraisal becoming a form-filling event. Its participative approach makes the appraisal feel more formative than summative, but the very openness is unnerving to staff who are new to appraisal. It suits mature, confident, able and willing staff who are used to the appraisal process.

The support checklist, however, has its own advantages. It may be called a directed appraisal because it directs the teacher's attention to key aspects of the job and key functions. It facilitates standardization of approach, which is important if staff are to see appraisal as fair. Each item on the list can be explained in detail by referral to the teacher's basic-task description. It is therefore easy to be specific when suggesting that a teacher should improve in any aspect of basic-task performance because the basic-task description lists the expected contribution. For example, a teacher not making an adequate contribution to the department might be expected to improve in one of the following ways:

- Know well the department's syllabus, organization and equipment.
- Make positive written suggestions about the continuing development of the department.
- Plan and accept responsibility for at least two long units of work for the department (i.e., work for one class for half a term) each year.
- Accept and execute at least two additional responsibilities each year (e.g., administration, stock, stationery, set lists) within the department as agreed with the head of department.

The danger for which heads and appraisers should be vigilant is that this system may encourage teachers to concentrate solely on the assessed areas on the checklist. On the other hand, a well-designed checklist will ensure that the school has all its staff aiming for common responsibilities and standards. The checklist will seek only for standards of performance and not influence or sterotype personal factors such as styles of teaching.

Each teacher and appraiser has a copy of the support checklist and each indicates before an appraisal meeting any aspect of the teacher's performance which he or she feels should be discussed.

The teacher may be concerned about classroom management and the discipline of a particular class; the appraiser may be concerned about complaints from pupils and parents on the quality of homework marking. Although it is certain that both topics would have been discussed and acted upon as they arose (remember, there should be no surprises at the appraisal interview) now is the time to look back over the problems which have occurred in the year. It is often an aid to discussion if both parties bring to the interview in this way their written ideas about any part of the checklist they wish to discuss. Following the interview it should be possible to make an agreed joint narrative statement on any aspect of the teacher's performance which causes specific concern to the teacher or the appraiser.

Written narrative reports limit the misunderstanding which sometimes arises between teacher and appraiser if the discussion of an aspect of poor performance causes the appraiser some embarrassment. This embarrassment can cause lack of clarity as in the following feedback to a teacher,

'I'm not very happy about you. I'd like you to buck up and do something about it. It's time you pulled yourself together. I think you know what I mean, Miss Dorkins.' The appraiser was sure his colleague had clearly understood where her performance fell short whereas Miss Dorkins was left wondering what was needed.

The detailed handling of the appraisal interview is the subject of Chapter 4, but the general rules for handling checklist appraisal are:

- Remember you are appraising the performance not the person.
- Be specific and give examples of aspects of the performance which give concern.
- Agree on action to remedy the performance faults, being as specific about the targets as possible.
- Acknowledge the parts of the performance which have been satisfactory.
- Thank the teacher for the work done.

Two further points need to be made about the use of checklists, both of which encourage professional development. These are the role of self-appraisal and the role of self-monitoring.

SELF-APPRAISAL AND SELF-MONITORING

Self-appraisal

Even with closely defined principal accountabilities, there is much scope for individual professional judgement. The varied nature of a task which requires the teacher to manage the education and development of many children makes it almost impossible to identify all possible situations and outcomes and to prescribe appropriate action. More importantly, detailed describing of these processes removes professional judgement on the part of the teacher so stunting the development of maturity. In fact the mature professional, when treated as an unable, inexperienced or unwilling person, tends to regress into that mode of operating and increasingly requires every action to be specified. 'If it isn't my job description, I don't do it' epitomizes the most unsuitable attitude we could expect from any professional person who is overmanaged in this way. For reasons, therefore, both of professional development and of expediency in a situation which has many contingencies, part of the appraisal process should be self-appraisal.

In the target-setting and appraisal system, self-appraisal is the first step in the appraisal process. Each teacher is given a warm-up document which asks the appraisee, amongst other things, to reflect upon the positive and negative features of the period of the school-performance year being appraised. Specific questions are asked about aspects of the teacher's performance of which he or she is pleased and proud as well as about aspects found to be difficult or dealt with unsatisfactorily. The warm-up document is examined in more detail in Chapter 5, but its chief purposes are clear. It encourages the teacher to identify his or her own strengths and weaknesses whether or not they are considered key-result areas by the school. Since a teacher often operates in situations where he or she is the only adult present and where the appraiser has to rely mainly on the teacher's interpretation, self-appraisal of some form must be developed. C. Margarison (1976) presents arguments in favour of self-appraisal in a further situation which can be related especially to senior staff in secondary schools, that is, when the teacher is the subject expert and the appraiser is not. This occurs frequently when a head or deputy is appraising the work of a head of department. Few heads have the expertise to do anything but rely on forms of self-appraisal in most curriculum areas, although in difficulty or dispute, the LEA probably has an equivalent subject specialist in the form of an adviser. Called in to assist, the subject adviser can be useful on technical matters or in giving a second opinion should teacher or appraiser need it. Another use for self-appraisal is in assessing contribution to a team task. At times when it is difficult for anyone outside the team to appraise an individual's performance within the team, self-appraisal, especially if shared with the self-appraisal by other team members, will produce a realistic assessment.

Finally, self-appraisal has been effective in the role it has unwittingly played in schools. Because few of the self-appraisal schemes introduced by LEAs even hint that a more structured appraisal system might follow, these safe, friendly, optional schemes stimulate interest in professional appraisal and development. They prepare teachers for a discussion of performance, for counselling and for improvement, and have done the same for their appraisers. Those heads and senior staff who fear more rigorous teacher appraisal are encouraged to initiate self-appraisal schemes and to build from these a more structured appraisal system.

In target setting and appraisal self-appraisal is a part of the process. Its precise importance will vary with the appraisal scheme and indeed in some it assumes overriding importance. The authors of the least hierarchical schemes advocate that teacher control of their evaluation is crucial. True self-evaluation, such schemes believe, is entirely in the hands of the evaluated, and the teacher should be free to chose the: aims; methods; evidence; and actions to take as a result.

It is difficult to believe that such schemes could make an effective contribution to performance improvement towards organizational goals.

The scope is great for a teacher to continue with a professional contribution the main aim of which is to bring satisfaction to the performer.

In general, self-appraisal has the following key disadvantages:

1. It is only halfway there. In itself it is not a sufficient source of data viewing a performance from only one perspective.
2. It is difficult to be objective about oneself. Appraisal can be a rare opportunity to see ourselves as others see us. Self-appraisers are frequently too hard on themselves and need praise, support and understanding to avoid being discouraged. Some self-appraisers, perhaps through immaturity, overvalue their own performances and need help to put their contribution into perspective.
3. Realistic improvement plans are difficult to make for the self-appraiser. Most development plans need the help, advice and understanding of the school or some of its staff to enhance the efficacy of in-service training, special projects and the like and to help to assess their success.

Self-monitoring

Self-monitoring is a practice that all but the most unwilling and unable teachers can achieve. Teacher and appraiser must agree upon the tasks and performance standards required so that the teacher may use the same criteria as the appraiser. Self-monitoring encourages both professional development and motivation. Professional development is enhanced and the teacher and appraiser discuss and agree upon the criteria for assessment, as well as from the self-monitoring process itself. Confidence grows because the teacher does not need to wait for feedback from the appraiser to know that the mission is being accomplished. Motivation is increased because most teachers would wish to progress in this form of appraisal and maintain a self-monitoring role. Self-monitoring can be used equally well in the team situation of a small school or in a department within a larger school.

THE ROLE OF CLASSROOM OBSERVATION IN TEACHER APPRAISAL

It is not difficult to set out in a job description the basic tasks required of a teacher in the classroom. These will probably relate to preparation of lessons, classroom management, safety of pupils, setting and marking of work, evaluation of pupils achievements and awareness of their problems and personalities. These aspects of classroom performance can be more fully defined, and teachers in adhering to them will produce a sound performance.

Yet, because we do now know how children learn it is almost impossible to produce a job description for effective teaching. As James Britton (1969) says, 'If the teacher could be more certain what learning looked like, he might find it easier to monitor his own teaching.' No outsider, however close to pupils, teacher or the subject, can make a judgement about a lesson to match that of the effective teacher. As Liz Thomson says:

> Central to our development has been the notion of teachers as participant observers. As a participant observer, the teacher is immediately aware of all the fine contextual details which can skew and bias the observations of outsiders. A teacher's total involvement and knowledge of the classroom context means that he or she is able to bring that knowledge to bear on any sort of judgement about the teaching and the learning taking place [Thomson and Thomson, 1984].

The quality of a lesson cannot be assessed merely by watching it.

Add to this other logistical difficulties of classroom observation. Do we observe all the classes a teacher may teach in a year? Do we watch all lessons? In all subjects? If not, how is the selection made? Do we see all of the lessons in a topic sequence? If not, how typical are the ones we observe? Do we see the teacher display all the classroom skills, from exposition to class discussion, to group teaching and individual coaching? If not how incomplete and distorted will our observations be? If we observe a previously nominated lesson how typical will that lesson be? It seems likely that the classroom observation of a scatter of the lessons which a teacher will teach in a year will be too few, too random and too distorted by the presence of the observer to be a satisfactory role-judge of teacher-classroom performance.

Each appraiser needs to identify a range of other devices with which to support a limited amount of classroom observation. These other devices should be explained to the teacher as sources of information which will be fed into any discussion of classroom performance. None will be sufficient in itself; most will need mutual trust and professional detachment in their interpretation. Taken raw or in isolation they could mislead, but used together and with an open, professional approach they would serve as useful guides to successful and unsuccessful performance areas. However, it would be wrong to give the impression that there is no role at all for classroom observation in teacher appraisal. The need for classroom observation becomes essential once it has been agreed between teacher and appraiser that a teaching problem has to be analyzed or a solution tested.

Take, for example, the case of Roy Dunn, a teacher of science of three years' experience, who barely passed his probationary year and has shown no sign of development. Whilst he was acceptable as a probationary teacher, his performance as a relatively experienced teacher is unsatisfactory. Each appraisal interview has led to a development programme in one or other of his weak areas. Notice that a problem existed was served by several parents' letters, pupil reaction to the possibility of Mr Dunn as a teacher, and departmental discussion of both the progress of his pupils and his care of equipment. Lesson observation and discussion with the teacher were set up to attempt to identify and isolate the contributory problems. These were felt to be in the three areas of clear exposition of the substance of a lesson, class control, and the organization of equipment and materials.

Further lesson observations followed by the appraiser, the head of science department, specifically to listen to the teacher's exposition and to advise and assist with improving the first of the problems of Mr Dunn's performance. As the teacher's explanation of the purpose and practices of the lesson improved, so did the second of his problems, class control. Nevertheless, observation by Mr Dunn of the head of department in action, followed by further discussion of class-control technique led to more classroom observation of the teacher. Formal lesson observation, it was felt, had a distorting effect upon class behaviour and so upon this aspect of performance. A more appropriate technique at that time was a series of brief visits to the lesson to give the appraiser a 'feel' of a few lessons. These impressions of lesson development were then fed back to the teacher to help him further improve his control techniques. The last of the three identified problems needed no lesson observation and was resolved by requiring the teacher to list his lesson materials one week in advance and to discuss the list with the head of department. This brief study illustrates that there is a strong case for classroom observation, not only as a general appraisal technique but for specific, identified purposes.

Our exploration of the appraisal process has brought us to a new definition of teacher appraisal: *Appraisal* is 'continuous feedbck on a teacher's performance towards agreed standards and targets, given by a colleague who is responsible for that teacher's peformance'. Anything else is dismissible.

The appraisal interview is the occasion when the continual appraisal of a teacher's performance is summarized.

Now let us summarize the teacher-appraisal process. The teacher's performance consists of a compulsory basic task and of optional targets. Target-appraisal criteria should be clearly identified at the time the targets are set. The basic task of a teacher is composed of certain principal accountabilities which the school must identify and convey to the teacher. The appraiser assesses the extent to which the basic task is carried out by collating feedback, by using a support checklist and through teacher self-appraisal and self-monitoring. The teacher is carefully inducted into the school so that its ethos also contributes to effective performance, to valued appraisal and to continuous supportive development.

4 THE APPRAISAL INTERVIEW

> Legislation is proposed to enable the Secretary of State in appropriate circumstances to require local education authorities to appraise the performance of their teachers [DES, 1985a].

The appraisal interview is an essential feature of any effective appraisal system. If appraisal is the continual forming of judgements about a performance, then the appraisal interview is the occasion when these judgements and the action taken as a result of them throughout the year are reviewed.

But appraisal interviewing should be built into the system if it is to happen at all. Appraisers may avoid the interview if allowed a choice. Rosemary Stewart confirms this from her industrial experience and says of appraisal interviews,

> Unless these interviews are official policy, few managers will initiate such a discussion with their subordinates since they may find it embarrassing to talk about a man's career, especially about his weaknesses. Still fewer subordinates will do so even if the manager has an open-door policy [Stewart, 1963].

The appraisal interview is also the most influential feature of an appraisal system. Even when colleagues have doubts or suspicions about the system, the interview can remove these by the manner in which it is conducted. It should be a joint review between two experts on a particular performance, the teacher who carried out the performance and the appraiser who carries ultimate responsibility for it. But the interview must be more than this joint review of past performance; it must also be concerned with how things might be done better in the future. A badly conducted appraisal can be a thoroughly demotivating experience, souring relationships and adversely affecting future performance. A successfully handled appraisal can bring the reverse — an improved relationship and a better performance. The essential purpose of an appraisal interview is to decide upon an action plan for the improvement of performance.

PREPARING FOR AN APPRAISAL INTERVIEW

To conduct an appraisal interview an appraiser should be properly trained in the skills of the interviewing and counselling of teachers. A training scheme is given in Chapter 7. The appraiser should fully understand the objectives of performance appraisal in general and of the school or LEA appraisal scheme in particular. Appraisal system design is the subject of Chapter 5. The appraiser also needs a realistic timetable for completing the interviews, their preparation and their follow up. The appraisal and target-setting year is discussed in Chapter 2, but the spread of interviews should ensure that no more than one per day is undertaken. Time of day, location and room preparation also need to be considered.

Time of day

The appraisal interview is not an optional extracurricular activity to be undertaken at the immediate end of a strenuous day's teaching. To allow both participants to be fairly fresh, interviews are best undertaken within the school day and it may be that staff would need to be relieved of teaching for this important activity. If outside the school day suits both participants best, leave a reasonable interval after teaching to relax and warm to the appraisal activity.

Location

The ideal location is a small office. If neither participants has a permanent one then borrow the use of an office for the period of the appraisal. As the practice of teacher appraisal grows in Britain, appraisers are frequently found trying to conduct appraisals in what they believe to be relaxed, informal surroundings off the school site such as pubs and restaurants. Appraisals are part of the official business of the school and should have the use of its best on-site facilities.

The teacher has to be given about ten days' notice of interview and encouraged to prepare for it by completing or at least considering three documents, a form of warm-up document, a basic task checklist and a copy of last year's targets. The teacher should be asked to review his or her work over the past year and any targets that were set. These documents between them will raise almost all the issues that the appraisal interview has to cover.

In Chapter 3 it is advocated that both self-appraisal and self-monitoring based on agreed criteria be used. To help with self-appraisal the teacher is usually given a preparatory or warm-up document. This document is discussed in detail in Chapter 5 but its general aims for the purpose of the interview are to encourage:

- Reflection on job performance by the teacher. Few of us have time to reflect on our work, but the questions and suggestions on the document help to focus attention on aspects of last year's performance
- Self-appraisal in areas where the teacher is the best or sole judge of performance
- Feedback from teacher to appraiser on problem areas
- Recognition and acknowledgement of successes by the teacher
- Acknowledgement by the teacher of support received from colleagues

An example of such a document is given in Chapter 5. The teacher is given the document at least ten days before the interview. Frequently this document is treated as the teacher's property with the option of:

- Completing it and giving a copy to the appraiser before or at the interview
- Retaining it during the interview as a form of crib sheet adding to it during the interview if necessary, and giving a copy to the appraiser after the interview
- Using it during the interview and retaining it
- Not using it at all

The importance of this document is the encouragement it gives to the teacher to contribute to the appraisal. Few teachers would wish to commit themselves to written statements before the interview if there were no possibility of retraction. To serve its purpose of encouraging self-appraisal in specific areas, the teacher should retain control of the warm-up document and should be free to decide whether it is to form a permanent part of his or her school record. Areas which can be covered on the warm-up document are: career plan; the positive aspect of the past 12 months; the negative aspect of the past 12 months; and general comment on the school and its work.

If a teacher wishes to include the warm-up sheet in the school staff files, it would be subject to the same rules of confidentiality as other appraisal documents. Confidentiality is discussed in Chapter 7 on system design.

ROOM PREPARATION

There is no ideal room arrangement for an appraisal interview, but rather a need to keep in mind the aim of setting a suitable climate. Easy chairs may relax some teachers but might unsettle others; discussion across a desk whilst sitting in upright chairs is too formal for some but reassuring to others. Try to predict which arrangement puts the teacher most at ease. A useful working arrangement will probably require a desk close at hand to carry documents, job descriptions, note pads and the like, but not laid out to form a physical barrier between the participants. If the room is large enough to contain both informal and formal areas, let the teacher choose the arrangement if this is appropriate.

Interruptions to an appraisal interview can shatter the confidence of the interviewee, usually destroy atmosphere and generally devalue the importance of the occasion. Take the telephone off the hook or arrange not to take any calls. Put a Meeting in Progress notice on the door to prevent people coming in.

The appraiser has the same set of documents, but needs to research only two of them, the basic task checklist and the target-setting sheet for the year now ending. Through the year, based on day-to-day management, the appraiser's view of the teacher's performance will be formed slowly in the mind. During the final few weeks the appraiser will refine his or her view of that performance by final checks of any evidence which he or she will be able to present to the teacher. The forms of this evidence are discussed in Chapter 3. At this stage the organization's view of the teacher's performance is not fully formed or crystallized. That stage will be reached in the interview when the teacher and appraiser participate in discussion. The appraiser must again be warned not to introduce surprises into the interview. Frequent feedback on the positive and negative features of the teacher's performance will have given both participants a reliable insight into what will be the major issues of discussion. Possibly plans of action will be forming in their minds, but perhaps not. If, however, by the time the interview is over the appraiser and teacher have not produced a plan of action which must be followed to improve performance, then the interview will have failed in its purpose.

THE STRUCTURE OF AN APPRAISAL INTERVIEW

The basic structure of all work discussion can be usefully analyzed as setting the climate, opening the interview, exploring viewpoints, making a plan and finally closing the interview. Using this simple outline an appraisal interview could be structured as: setting the climate; opening the interview; exploration; performance review and analysis; individual needs and aspirations; future performance and targets; and closure.

SETTING THE CLIMATE

Begin an appraisal interview, as with any form of interview, by setting the climate in which the discussion is to take place. Appraisal interviews require a relaxed, receptive and confidential mood which is encouraged by some informal preliminaries. The offer of a cup of coffee or tea, the availability of an ashtray for smokers not only show normal politeness and respect but help to set a relaxed mood. A few pleasantries may be useful, although since this is to be a discussion with a colleague whom the appraiser probably knows well, it will be unnecessary to spend the amount of time needed at a selection interview to encourage conversation. David Warwick's (1983) booklet suggests that it is better to take the teacher to the interview room than to wait for him or her to arrive, but again the guideline is to suit the action to the teacher.

Next, it is for the appraisal interviewer to ensure that the appraiser and the teacher have the same perception of the purpose of the scheme. If the appraiser makes the explanation, allow the teacher time to question, summarize or clarify. Another technique is to ask the teacher to explain his or her perception of the purpose and to leave it to the appraiser to fill in any gaps in knowledge. The purpose of the scheme should be explained as the improvement of performance, adding any subsidiary purposes with which the teacher may be concerned. It also helps the teacher to know how the appraiser would like to structure the meeting, subject to any acceptable suggestions the teacher may make.

This part of the interview should take less than five minutes.

OPENING THE INTERVIEW

The aim of this short but important part of an appraisal interview is to focus the teacher's attention on the heart of the matter. Although only a minute or two is taken to do so it is important to remind the teacher both of the interview purposes and that this is not 'just another chat' but the annual appraisal interview. The purposes of the interview are to review the teacher's annual performance and to produce a programme for performance improvement including training needs. Something simple and direct will serve to open the interview, for example, 'The main aim of this interview is to look at your work performance over the past year in both the basic task and the targets we set. We both have a copy of the task and target sheet. What progress do you feel you made with the first item on the checklist in your role as tutor to C3?' This opening identifies the theme of the interview, outlines its general boundaries and opens up the interview to the teacher to present his or her perception of performance.

EXPLORATION: PEFORMANCE REVIEW AND ANALYSIS

The aim in this stage of the interview is to review the basic-task performance and the targets set for the past year and agree upon the extent to which they have been achieved. There will be an examination of the reasons for nonachievement or underachievement. Factors such as aptitude, learning, ability, motivation and attitude as well as unavoidable external factors will be considered. Both teacher and appraiser contribute their views of performance since the last appraisal. As an agenda, use the support checklist with its list of principal task accountabilities and make an observation on each principal area, since this gives feedback in stages.

Be as specific as possible and explain on what evidence a judgement is being made. Bring out negative and positive comments as they appear. Do not save all the 'bad news' to follow the 'good news'. Encourage the teacher to comment on the evidence the appraiser produces. Ask the teacher open and closed questions about his or her own feelings on performance in each of these key areas. Use reflective questions to encourage the teacher to present a viewpoint. Remember the teacher has already considered his or her own performance in these areas and has a copy of the same support checklist which the appraiser is using. Be prepared to show flexibility in the light of new information which is presented in the meeting. As a variation in technique ask the teacher to give his or her view on each of the support-checklist items before the appraiser comments. There is no preferred method of handling this aspect of appraisal, but the aim must be to discuss the support checklist in a full, open and frank way, summarizing a conclusion on each of the principal accountabilities and on any proposed action.

It rests with the appraiser to keep the tone of the interview positive and look towards future improvement in performance. Even in areas of unsatisfactory performance there is little point on dwelling on the past once it is acknowledged that there is a problem except to analyze why it exists. Be prepared to present the source as well as the feedback. Say 'I saw' or 'The deputy head is worried' instead of 'you are'. You are presenting evidence for discussion not a predetermined judgement over which the teacher has no control. Remember the purpose of the interview is to produce a plan for future improvement.

The appraiser should be prepared at any stage for the teacher to indicate obstacles to an improved performance. Encourage dialogue on how these obstacles can be removed. Be especially prepared that you as appraiser may through aspects of your own performance be an obstacle to the teacher's development. It may require greater maturity on the appraiser's part than most aspects of the appraisal process but the teacher should be encouraged to say what he or she would like the appraiser to do differently.

The next stage of interview continues with an appraisal of targets. If the advice on target setting is followed there will be little problem in agreeing on their achievement.

INDIVIDUAL NEEDS AND ASPIRATIONS

Next comes the opportunity for the teacher to introduce aspects of his or her work which may have so far been overlooked. The basis for this is the warm-up document which the teacher has completed. In particular it allows the teacher to discuss short- and long-term career plans, and any special preparation or coaching which the school could provide to help these plans along. These career decisions belong to the teacher, but the interview is an opportunity to tell the appraiser, who can act as a catalyst, or as test of realism and can counsel, guide and support.

The warm-up document will also have encouraged the teacher to reflect on his or her greatest successes over the year and to have indicated which gave greatest satisfaction. But the same document also encourages the teacher to discuss the least successful aspects of the year's work, any weakness in technical or managerial competence and any skills of the teacher which have not been well used by the school. Inevitably this will lead to suggestions for development and improvement, which is the theme of the next stage of the appraisal interview. In this part of the interview, however, the teacher has been encouraged to offer a personal and professional opinion, to expose any problem areas and areas of achievement and to discuss training needs.

Stop at this stage and summarize the past year's performance before going on to discuss the future. In the case of each aspect of the basic task and of each of the targets which have not been achieved the cause is sought and remedies produced in the form of new or reset targets. When they have been achieved the appraiser must use the occasion to show his or her own appreciation and the appreciation of the school. Celebration of a task achieved is an important feature of the appraisal interview.

FUTURE PERFORMANCE AND TARGETS

In this stage, the appraiser and the teacher look towards future performance. How will any weaknesses which have been identified be strengthened? How will inexperience be turned to experience? How will missing skills be acquired? The scheme at this stage is entirely concerned with staff development. Teacher and appraiser should feel free to suggest appropriate development activities. Some, from the time of the meeting, can become firm plans, but others which need discussion with colleagues are applications for courses, reallocation of resources, or the like and will still be proposals. In these cases the only firm plans will concern agreement on who is responsible for taking the next steps, how progress will be reported, when the plan will be formulated and reviewed.

Earlier in the interview the teacher may have suggested a career plan or, at least, the proposed next career step. Can the appraiser arrange for development which will help in this direction? Is it possible to create opportunities which benefit the school and the teacher at the same time? For example, does the school need someone to manage a 'Computers in the Curriculum' project at the same time that a teacher is looking for experience as a team leader and an opportunity to use Information Technology skills on a basis wider than that of a single department?

Consider teacher development to be a wide concept and ask what the specific purpose of any proposed training is to be. Is it to develop new skills, faster responses in existing skills or to change outdated skills? Is it to gain new knowledge and understanding or to become familiar with new routines? Is it to change attitudes and conditioned responses? Although there is a role for external courses, by far the most important part of staff development is learning in the job situation. Consider in-school learning tasks and methods such as:

Preparing reports, papers and reviews
Giving talks to colleagues, parents, governors
Leading/sharing in discussion
Guided reading
Leading/sharing in a project
Role playing
Simulation
Practice under supervision
Observation of good practice
Discussion of case studies
Sharing in group exercises
Understudy training
Special assignments
Coaching
Job rotation or temporary job change
Job sharing
Keeping a log
Using a checklist
Regular reporting and feedback on progress

Be careful not to suggest a development activity merely as a bribe. Adopt a method of learning which meets the training need. The target which involves a school-based project is an admirable learning device and has been mentioned earlier. In this mode of learning

(a) The school can set a task which fulfils an organizational need.

(b) The project remains within school control. It can be revamped, reduced, ended or extended with little effect outside the school itself.

(c) The success of the project can be assessed because the staff involved and the work itself remain within school.

(d) It can provide a satisfying challenge for the teacher, bringing more in status than being 'sent on a course'.

(e) If a new teacher-pay structure brings flexible funding, there could be temporary upgrading in salary during the period of a particularly onerous project.

Each time a target is set, leave no room for possible misunderstandings or for erroneous assumption. Use the target-setting criteria which were discussed earlier. In particular remember that good action plans should be:

1. Measurable: 'Increase the percentage of parents attending school reporting evenings' **not** 'Improve parental support of the school.'
2. Specific: 'Make 200 new flashcards by the end of term' **not** 'Make a significant increase in the stock of flashcards in the department.'
3. Realistic/attainable: Motivation to do something is to a large extent determined by the expectation we have of succeeding. Overambitious objectives can lead to frustration and disillusionment.
4. Time bonded: 'Implement the new computer system by March 31' **not** 'Get the system in as soon as possible.'

At this stage, the target-setting system has come full circle as the appraiser and teacher find themselves setting targets once more.

CLOSURE

Finally the interview reaches its formal closure. At this time:

- Make sure there is nothing else the teacher wants to tell you or to discuss. Is there some matter the teacher lacked the confidence to raise early in the interview, or even to note on the warm-up document? 'Is there any other matter at all that you would like to discuss?' confirms that the appraiser has tried to make this as comprehensive and open a meeting as possible for the teacher.
- Make sure that targets and their criteria are clear and agreed. The teacher or appraiser could compile the written targets, but it is more usual for the appraiser to do this with the teacher agreeing to them. However, it adds further challenge to many teachers to write their own targets following an appraisal interview and target-setting discussion and to pass them to the appraiser for agreement.
- Make sure the teacher is thanked for his or her contribution to the school. The appraiser will have spent much of the interview discussing how performance can be improved and can give the impression of having overlooked that major part of performance which has been at least satisfactory and may have been superb. The appraiser should be willing to show his or her own interest and excitement at the challenge the teacher faces in the year ahead. Surely the discussion has done something to 'turn on' the appraiser as well as the appraised.

Walk the teacher to the door, shake hands and return to the final part of the appraisal interview process, the follow up.

AFTER THE INTERVIEW

The purpose of the appraisal interview is to produce a plan for improved teacher performance. Having agreed and recorded that plan in the interview you have it typed and a copy sent as soon as possible to those directly concerned. In most appraisal systems there are the appraisee, the appraiser and the appraiser's appraiser — the teacher, the head of department and the headteacher in most medium to large schools. If the appraiser agreed to take some action it should be taken quickly or noted for early reference.

Be sure that any commitments made in the appraisal interview are carried through. Applications for off-site courses for skills training or for general information and awareness should be made without delay. Promises of in-school development opportunities, such as new responsibilities, on the job training or the like, should be fulfilled. Weak points in a teacher's performance should receive the observation and analysis agreed in the interview. This is the opportunity to arrange to use lesson observation to the full, as a means of identifying and analyzing a teaching weakness. Close observation of all staff in action is neither feasible nor desirable, but helping a colleague to improve may well need close and continual monitoring.

If there were minor disagreements on the basic-task performance which are not to be the subject of targets, these might be noted. Any major difference of opinion on the basic task would have formed a large part of the interview and inevitably resulted in a target.

Next, record other useful information which came to light in the interview — a changed career aspiration, a new academic interest — or indeed any change in personal circumstances which might have a bearing on job performance or career development.

Lastly make a note in the 'Bring Up' diary to review progress at the date agreed during the meeting.

Now the interview and its follow-up are completed it is time to ask how successful the appraiser felt it was. One industrial company suggests these questions:

Was the interview an open and constructive discussion?
Has the appraiser gained a greater understanding of his or her staff?
Are the targets of each colleague clear?
Have the teacher's expectations of the appraisal system and the interview been met?

Performance appraisal is a great motivator, a powerful means of communication and a means of producing more effective schools. There is no more important item in the whole appraisal process than the appraisal interview.

A CHECKLIST FOR APPRAISERS

1. Plan what you want to achieve from the appraisal interview: If the interview goes well what will have been achieved by the end of it?
2. Prepare for the appraisal: Have you drawn together all the information you need on the teacher being appraised?
3. Be sure of privacy: Have you made as certain as you can that you will not be interrupted by people or by telephone calls?
4. Seating arrangements: Are the chairs in the position you want? Do you want to give the teacher a choice of seating arrangements?
5. Planning the time: Have you allowed enough time before your next commitment?
6. Planning the structure of the appraisal interview: Have you made an outline plan for the appraisal interview?
7. Consider opening the appraisal interview: How will you open the interview so that you will put the teacher at ease?
8. Establishing an appropriate relationship: How participative do you want to be?
9. Sharing the interview: Are you prepared to use listening skills for a high percentage of the appraisal interview?
10. Pooling information: Have you got all the facts and information you may need to give?
11. Asking the appropriate questions: Have you prepared some open-ended questions to allow the teacher to expand on a point of view?
12. Exploration of feelings: Are you prepared to allow the teacher to express feelings as well as facts?
13. Agreement in the appraisal interview: Are you ready to summarize in writing the agreed courses of action?
14. Closing the appraisal interview: Have you thought about how you will finish the interview?
15. Taking appropriate action: Are you ready to follow up the interview with action you promised to take and check that the teacher does the same?

LISTENING SKILLS

The balance of 'air time' averaged over an appraisal interview should be that the teacher takes 70% and the appraiser 30%. Looked at another way, the appraiser is listening for 70% of the time.

The most obvious way to conduct an interview yet let the teacher do most of the talking is by effective questioning. Most school staff will be aware from their classroom work of the need to use closed questions, which can be answered more quickly than they can be asked, only occasionally to check understanding or to bring a wandering interview back to its task. Instead, use more frequently those open questions which include the words *who*, *which*, *where*, *why*, *what* and *how*. For example,

Who has contributed to . . . ?
Which are your strongest skills in the classroom?
Where would be suitable locations for this project?
Why do you feel that way about . . . ?
What were the problems . . . ?
How could that situation be improved?

Such questions encourage the teacher to express his or her real thoughts, views, impressions and help to build trust and commitment.

Listening is a skill. How is it done well? It may be trite to advise an appraiser to begin by sitting in a position which suggests interest in the teacher's contribution, that is, facing the teacher and leaning slightly forward. Eye contact is crucial especially when important stages are being reached, as too are facial expression and gesture. We are all aware that it is possible to listen without appearing to do so, but to encourage discussion it should be obvious that the appraiser is listening.

There is no hypocrisy in using the listening techniques and no substitute for genuine listening. The techniques only reassure the teacher that the appraiser is doing so. Other actions which help the discussion along and confirm the appraiser's attention are:

1. Testing understanding: Does that mean you were not able to attend the course as you had arranged?
2. Summarizing: So now we have reviewed all of your classes for last year except the 'O' level English group . . .
3. Supporting: Yes, I think your idea is a good one.
4. Reflecting: *Teacher.* I would really like to improve my academic qualifications.
   Appraiser. Improve your academic qualifications?

Effective listening can mean more than listening to the actual meaning of the words spoken. Try to listen for what is left unsaid. Look for a hidden meaning by watching the facial expression as the discussion develops. Consider pauses and hesitation. Is the teacher trying to tell you something which needs your further encouragement to develop?

Another aspect of listening technique is to watch for 'body language'. Sometimes the gesture, posture and body movement of the teacher in interview can hint that there is more to be added in the discussion.

Listening is not merely 'not talking'. It is searching the conversation of the teacher to let that decide what the next question will be. Empathy is more likely to be established through the effective use of listening skills than through any other aspect of appraisal interviewing.

STYLE IN THE APPRAISAL INTERVIEW

The most widely used style in an appraisal interview is a participative, problem-solving one in which both teacher and appraiser present their evidence and feelings on the teacher's performance and both seek ways of supporting continued improvement and development. The aim is to encourage such growth both through correcting faults in the performance and through the discussion of job-related problems. The appraiser appears as not only the teacher's manager but counsellor, helper and facilitator. The discussion itself is intended to generate new ideas to support those which both participants brought to the appraisal interview.

The skills required in the effective use of such a style are those needed to draw out and encourage trust in the teacher. Open exploratory questions, the ability to reflect the teacher's ideas and feelings accurately and an ability to listen effectively are all important. So too is an ability to synthesize and summarize, to show understanding and to draw the discussion towards a course of action or target. Success requires both trust and a willingness on the part of the teacher to participate in problem solving. If there is some penalty in disclosing that a fault or a problem exists in performing why would a teacher not continue to conceal it? The appraiser wants the teacher to be motivated by the sense of freedom to identify problems, by the sense of responsibility for finding solutions, by an intrinsic interest in being able to tackle a job more effectively and by the possibility of the interest and support of the appraiser.

Although this mode of managing change is slowed if the teacher is too cautious in offering ideas — about why performance goes wrong or about how to put it right — ideas and solutions originated by the teacher are to be encouraged. There is some risk for the appraiser that the teacher may be more highly motivated towards a change in a part of the teaching performance which the appraiser may not value as highly as some other change. Nevertheless, the open and frank discussion will increase mutual respect, and a development programme the teacher can accept will result. Unless the basic-task performance has failed to reach a satisfactory standard there is no point forcing a development programme on a teacher. Persuasion and encouragement are legitimate: manipulation is not. In the final analysis, the appraiser cannot motivate the teacher: people motivate themselves.

With an unsatisfactory feature of the basic task, however, it cannot be left to the teacher to decide whether to improve. The appraiser must present the evidence of what is going wrong to convince the teacher that a problem exists. The kinds of evidence which can be presented to the teacher are listed in Chapter 3. They should always include specific examples of the unsatisfactory behaviour and the source of information, whether from the appraiser from clients or from colleagues. Preferably these examples should be written. They should indicate trends or repeated poor performance and should be distinguished from the single aberration which the teacher learns never to repeat. With repeated unsatisfactory performance, the teacher clearly has not learned and has to 'own' the problem to work effectively for its solution. This stage of the discussion, when the appraiser is trying to convince the teacher that a problem exists and that it is the teacher's problem, well repays any time spent on it. Success is more likely when the teacher respects and trusts the appraiser but if in the final resort the appraiser finds that neither a participative nor a 'selling' style convince the teacher that an aspect of performance in the basic task is unsatisfactory then telling is all that remains as a choice of style. This 'telling' mode is best suited to those who lack either the ability or the willingness to perform well, although remedy in each of those cases may be vastly different.

IMPROVING THE UNSATISFACTORY PERFORMANCE

The first stage in any improvement programme is the recognition that the problem exists (see Figure 4). Usually, in a sensitive atmosphere of trust, staff are willing to discuss their weaknesses as they see them. This discussion of the teacher's performance may:

1. Confirm problems known to the teacher and the appraiser
2. Uncover weaknesses which the teacher sees as problems but which are not seen as such by the school
3. Expose weaknesses of which the school is aware, but the teacher is not

The first category of problem is the easiest with which to deal. In a trusting, positive atmosphere various courses of action to improve performance can be explored and formulated. Action may be needed by the appraiser or the teacher or both and a range of possibilities should be explored. The teacher is more likely to follow an improvement plan which he or she has helped to formulate, and more so if it is the teacher who is anxious to follow it and who is responsible for the outcome. In a school this improvement programme could be an increased contribution to the stock of department resources (a set of worksheets, a series of year tests, a computer program), but it could as easily be improved personal performance (greater promptness at lessons, better relationships with departmental colleagues, more accurate recording of pupil grades). The whole range

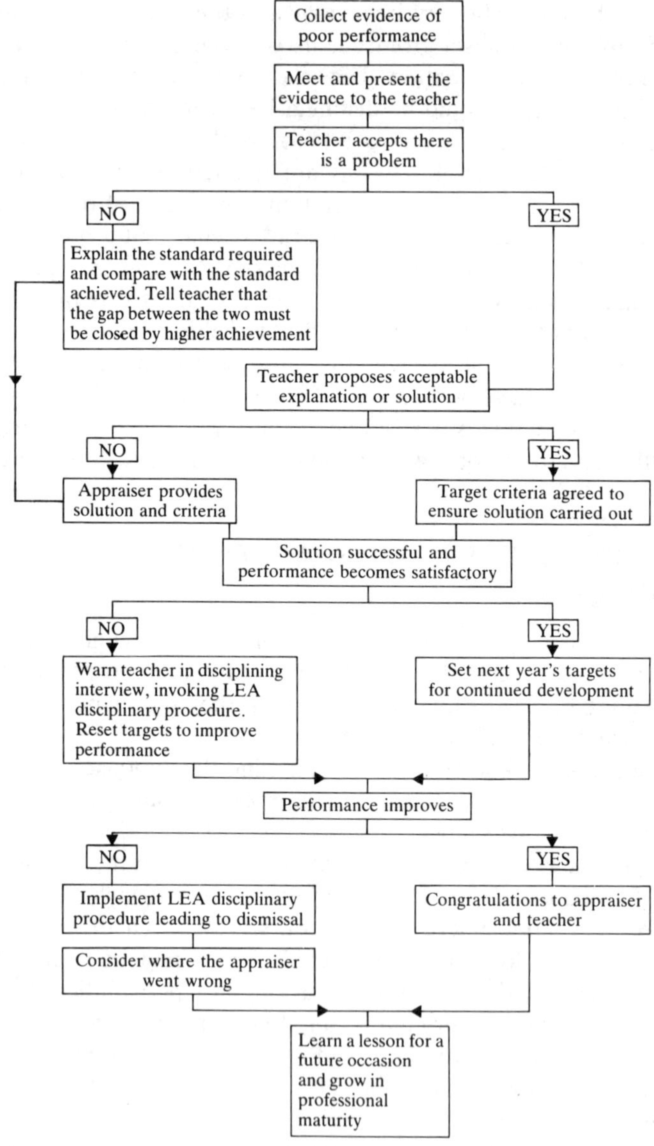

Figure 4 Handling an unsatisfactory teacher performance

of personal and professional improvements can be explored, the alternative courses of action identified with the teacher helping to decide which route to improve performance should be followed.

The second category of problem — the teacher sees a problem where the school does not — requires patience and sensitive listening skills. The appraiser must be able to see the teacher's point of view and understand it, even if the appraiser does not agree with it. Possibly there is no problem for the school at all. A teacher may, for example, feel that his or her discipline needs to be improved because of a comparison with the more authorative style used by the teacher next door. Clarifying the criteria by which we would assess good and bad discipline may reassure the teacher that there is no organizational problem there at all.

Another form of this same problem, in which the teacher is aware of a problem but the appraiser is not, may be due to a weakness in the appraiser's performance. This phenomenon is examined in more detail later in this chapter from the teacher's viewpoint. The appraiser should be prepared for the possibility that his or her performance may come under discussion. If so, do not spend time defending and arguing; devote the energy to understanding fully what is being said, sometimes even 'between the lines'. Reflect back feelings to ensure that you have understood: So, John, if I published the calendar of school dates by May for the forthcoming academic year, that would give you more time to plan your year? Alison, you feel you are not supported in disciplinary cases? Why do you feel you are not being given the professional development opportunities which I give to others, Harry? In these cases the appraiser needs all the honest feedback available if he or she is to be the one to improve in performance.

In the third category of interview the greatest problem is to have the teacher acknowledge and face up to a problem. Here the teacher is genuinely or apparently unaware that his or her performance is of concern. It is perfectly possible that a teacher believes that the standard of discipline or of homework or the level of contribution to departmental activities or the quality of administrative work which he or she is producing is what the school requires. Effective induction techniques for new staff and regular appraisals would make it difficult to accept that any member of staff would be left for long in that state of blissful ignorance. Nevertheless, no improvement programme can be effective until the teacher can acknowledge that a problem exists. That stage of making the teacher aware of a performance shortfall can be a traumatic one for all concerned but must nonetheless be faced.

Having identified an aspect of unsatisfactory or poor performance, the next step is to isolate the cause of that performance and the final aspect is to agree on a solution. Much depends on whether the teacher is not performing well because of inability or because of unwillingness. Is the teacher saying 'I can't do better' or 'I won't do better'? If the cause is related to inability, continue to explore the reasons which might be:

- Lack of knowledge: This may be of an aspect of a subject discipline. Perhaps the teacher is not teaching in his or her specialism or has not kept up to date with changing knowledge. It may relate to a school routine or to some other job requirement. Maybe the problem could be swiftly resolved if the teacher knew to whom to turn for help in the school.
- Lack of skill: Teaching, testing, coaching pupils or controlling and motivating them. Maybe the missing skill is a personal one, such as an inability to prepare effectively, to organize work or to remember. Maybe too, such skill omission is the fault of poor training and possibly poor selection that a teacher without these qualities was appointed to the school.
- Too much pressure: Stress is a stimulus up to a point, for example, in preparing a class to reach a standard of performance. Beyond that point when other preparing, teaching, marking possibly together with personal problems from home occur, teaching performance with that formerly challenging class may deteriorate. The teacher becomes irritable, vindictive, aggressive, unjust as he or she tries to fight the pressure or becomes hesitant, overcautious, ill or frequently absent from school in trying to run away from the pressure.
- Not enough personal challenge: This results in an unmotivated teacher. For example, the very able Scale 1 teacher who, with little prospect of in-service training or of promotion feels increasingly demotivated by the task. Motivation would come from prospects of improved status, promotion and personal growth.
- Financial: Another example may be that of badly paid teachers. Without the prospect of promotion they are hard to motivate because their efforts may be directed towards supplementing their salary through non-school work. Income to cover basic needs, such as the mortgage, food, transport, must for most people be certain before they can be motivated by belonging to a good department, by personal skills development or by prestige.
- Illness: Some teachers have illnesses they do not wish others to know about. Some have known illnesses and feel able to continue working, but by unofficially adjusting the level of performance. This adjustment may be in the form of increased absence or being less effective in the classroom or

less efficient with school administration. For the malingerer, peer-group pressure is usually an effective antidote; for the genuinely ill a frank discussion, perhaps involving the LEA Medical Officer, may result in a compromise working arrangement.

• The working environment: Some teachers perform badly because they lack the appropriate materials, equipment or other resources to do better. Teaching science in a classroom is possible as is Physical Education without a gymnasium, but lack of such resources can make the task more difficult and frustrating for both the pupils and the teacher. Surprisingly small cost additions can improve performance such as better lighting, easier access to a telephone or cleaner, better decorated rooms. If we consider pupils to be part of the 'working environment', has the teacher been given a particularly difficult group or have new pupils joining made the group unacceptably large?

If the appraiser and teacher agree that there is an unsatisfactory performance and the teacher now wants to raise that performance to reach an agreed satisfactory standard, then the next step is work together on the cause of the poor performance. Remember three practical guidelines:

1. Give feedback often: Formal appraisal interviews may be taking place only once or twice a year. Feedback based on actual instances (a letter from a parent, a set of comparative test results, a report which missed a school 'deadline' date) given as they arise will have best effect. Small changes in the short term add up to a big change in the long term.
2. Teachers are people: Imagine yourself in the teacher's position before you begin a counselling interview. Understand their personal circumstances, their personal values, but accept that you have the right to change their school performance. However, it is essential to self-improvement that the teacher retains his or her self-respect. Build it, do not destroy it.
3. It is not a personality change: Concentrate on behaviour which people can control. Neither appraisal nor counselling is intended to change personality. Focus on performance, not traits. Focus on ineffective job behaviour, based on incidents of which the head has specific examples which are legitimate and potentially fruitful areas for change.

When a programme is agreed, use all the target-setting criteria to ensure that there is no misunderstanding about what is intended to be achieved. Agree the dates of any follow up meetings and make it clear that the appraiser is giving time, energy and expertise to support the teacher's improvement. The appraiser needs to be firm yet supportive. Depending on how close the performance is to a disciplinary interview, the possible outcomes of failing to improve can be clarified. However, once the improvement has begun, frequent positive feedback is essential.

HOW THE TEACHER CAN WORK WITH AN UNSATISFACTORY APPRAISER

When a school decides that its senior and middle managers are to undertake appraisals it is often asking them to develop a skill and assume a responsibility which they did not expect to carry. For this reason alone it is unrealistic to expect that school staff will all quickly become skilled in appraisal techniques and some teachers may well find themselves being managed by an appraiser who is lacking in the necessary skill, willingness or ability. The unsatisfactory appraiser is often operating in one of nine style patterns.

1. The Defeated Appraiser: Knows that job definition, target setting and appraisal are difficult, and so believes they cannot really be achieved. Shirks appraisals situations. Misses deadline dates and meetings. Acts in a disspirited way.
2. The Bureaucratic Appraiser: Sets great store by accurate documentation. Becomes obsessed with paperwork at the expense of helping people or improving actual performance.
3. The Naive Appraiser: Discussions on performance are based entirely on feelings, relationships and goodwill. Little effort to identify areas for objective measurement or realistic professional judgement. Leaves the teacher without measures and standards which both parties can accept, so that appraisal is meaningless.
4. The Pedantic Appraiser: Expects to conduct an appraisal based upon objective evidence only. Leaves nothing to professional judgement or to subjectivity. Unable to accept that even objective criteria may require subjective interpretation, sometimes.
5. The Unfair Appraiser: Seeks to punish the teacher for other shortcomings which are outside the performance review. Pressurizes the teacher to accept unrealistic targets. Expects higher standards from one teacher than another for unjust reasons.
6. The Information Hoarder: No appraisal of staff and no personal feedback. No feedback on how the department is doing. No help with deciding priorities. Holds on to information which the teacher needs to perform well.
7. The Dictator: Uses a 'tell' style constantly, even with mature, experienced staff. Seldom delegates, never discusses decisions. Makes a great display of correcting a teacher's mistakes, so inhibiting initiative.
8. The Mouse: Shows no leadership to the department. Leaves teachers with little idea of how their work fits into the department. Never identifies staff responsibilities. Does little planning, directing or controlling of the department, leaving colleagues feeling lost.

9. The Two-faced Appraiser: Cannot be sure that what is said is what is meant. Responds to the most recent pressure. Frequently reverses decisions. Tends to give unjust reprimands, although the fault often lies with the appraiser's own unpredictability.

Being appraised by a leader with some of the nine problems can demotivate teachers and encourage their regression into styles in which they do not develop well professionally. A false relationship develops between teacher and appraiser and management is little more than a game. A question frequently put to those who lead courses in appraisal techniques concerns how teachers can deal with an unsatisfactory appraiser.

There are broadly three positive approaches to this stagnating state of affairs which may be classified as: help the appraiser to improve; be self-motivating; and take it to the appraiser's 'boss'.

HELP THE APPRAISER TO IMPROVE

To begin this approach, adopt the maxim 'Talk with me not about me.' The teacher should tell the appraiser what he or she feels is going wrong. With an ineffective appraiser, the habit grows of talking around an issue instead of talking openly with him or her about it. Maybe part of the problem is the teacher's fear of raising the matter; certainly this silence inhibits the search for a solution. Possibly airing the problem would lead to regular meetings devoted to bringing internal departmental problems out into the open and discussing them.

Appraisal is a two-way process. Explain what you, as a teacher, want from an appraiser and you may achieve it, thus improving not only the appraiser's performance but your own working environment.

Sharing information, such as articles, books, reports of courses, may revive a disspirited leader. A shared experience for the whole department such as a curriculum development or team-building exercise may be another means of expediting change.

If the problem is a lack of clarity of responsibilities and objectives, the teacher can outline his or her own interpretation of these and take them to the appraiser for agreement.

Another ploy is to look for delegation. Teachers could solve many problems within a department by offering to take delegated responsibility for an aspect of department management which at present is not being well handled. This may lighten the load for the appraiser and facilitate efficacy. It may leave the appraiser time to be a better planner or to identify challenges the department should be taking.

Giving the appraiser credit is another avenue to pursue. When an appraiser has worked particularly hard or done a good job in some way, try giving him or her some positive feedback. There is little enjoyment in managing people who are never grateful or appreciative. On the other hand leading a team of teachers who show their appraiser that they care about the pupils, about each other, about the work of the department and about their leader encourages development and change in a powerful way. Don't just talk about the appraisers bad habits, do something.

BE SELF-MOTIVATING

Most teachers will feel motivated after an effective appraisal interview. Although it is much more difficult to carry out a realistic appraisal oneself, it is possible to find sources of self-motivation. Personal pride, professional ambition, a caring concern for others can all provide the drive for a self-motivated performance. Maybe this will not be as effective as sharing, discussing and forming a good professional relationship with the appraiser, but it is a much better approach than regressing into a negative or immature attitude.

Self-motivation not only helps the teacher to maintain his or her own self-respect, but can, in turn, spur the tired appraiser back into action. A teacher who works hard, accepts responsibility, innovates and continues to develop can be a source of motivation to the appraiser.

TAKE IT TO THE APPRAISER'S 'BOSS'

If all else fails, and the appraiser's performance is inhibiting the development of the department and its staff, the teacher should identify the particular problem for the appraiser's appraiser. The opportunity to do this is presented at a grandfather or leapfrog interview, discussed earlier. No-one should see this as tale telling, but rather as a pooling of information on a school problem. This allows someone who is responsible for the appraiser's performance to set targets and monitor the ensuing improvement.

5 DESIGNING AND SETTING UP AN APPRAISAL SYSTEM

> Order is heaven's first law
>
> Alexander Pope

Most of those who are experienced in appraisal in other fields, find on examining the organization and structure of schools that they support

> the suggestion that schemes need to be created locally, that the national notion, although it may appear superficially to have some advantages, is actually disadvantageous in many ways because it fails to take into account the kind of local differences that we have all described [McKenzie, 1986].

Appraisal systems do not travel well: each school or LEA should design a system which meets its own particular needs. There is a temptation to import from schools which have the credibility of a tradition of successful staff appraisal, completely formed systems, routines and documentation. Appraisal systems are designed to achieve particular purposes, to suit particular organizations and to embody particular values. The first steps in designing an appraisal system are: identify the purpose of the system; and plan the organization of the system.

IDENTIFY THE PURPOSE OF THE SYSTEM

Much has already been said in Chapter 3 about the purposes of appraisal and the implications of setting up systems whose main aims are salary distribution, potential identification or performance improvement. None the less this primary aim must be identified. If the system is to have subsidiary aims for the school, the teacher or the LEA these too should be considered.

An example of such a statement of purpose might read as follows:

Main Purpose: Performance improvement

Subsidiary purposes from the viewpoint of the school

1. To plan guide and coordinate the work of teachers and departments
2. To develop teachers through on-the-job training
3. To obtain feedback for the school from its staff on all aspects of school development

Subsidiary purposes from the viewpoint of the teacher

1. To obtain feedback from an appraiser who is responsible for teacher performance
2. To contribute to and comment on school and departmental policy
3. To receive guidance and support in personal and professional development

Subsidiary purposes from the viewpoint of the LEA

1. To set up a system of conveying responsibilities and standards to teachers.
2. To assess needs for training and development and have feedback on its success

A system set up to meet these purposes will probably require, for example, appraisal interviews, job descriptions and a form of line management. It will probably not require, for example, a grading of teacher annual performance, forecasts of suitability for types of promoted posts, central pooling of detailed teacher-performance information. Features which do not help to meet its stated purpose should neither be added to the system nor even retained within it.

PLAN THE ORGANIZATION OF THE SYSTEM

Planning the structure and organization of an appraisal system is not an easy task. It may help to approach the task by using the following questions as a development plan:

1. Who is appraised?
2. Who appraises?
3. Is self-appraisal used?
4. Which period of performance is appraised?
5. What is to be the measure of performance?
6. Is there to be an appraisal interview?
7. Is there to be appraisal documentation?
8. What is to be done about future performance?
9. Is potential to be rated?
10. What is the relationship of appraisal to salary?

11. How often do appraisal interviews take place?
12. How is fairness maintained between teachers?
13. Is any appraisal information used centrally?
14. How confidential is the information?
15. Are there other uses for the appraisal information?

WHO IS APPRAISED?

Is the system intended to apply to all school staff — teaching, caretaking, ancillary personnel — or only to some? If appraisal brings benefits to the individual, why would the scheme not apply to all who contribute to the development of the school? If it is intended for teaching staff, will it apply to all whatever their scale and post? Many industrial appraisal schemes apply only to those who do not produce a measurable, physical product, such as those who manage others and whose performance achievements are therefore not as easily identified and assessed. There appears to be no case for making such a distinction with teachers. Some 'nonprofit motive' public-service industries such as police forces introduce a cut-off point for experienced officers beyond which it is believed little change is likely to take place. Designers of school-appraisal systems however may find it difficult to accept the philosophy that appears to resign itself to accepting that no change is possible in experienced teachers. Some otherwise intractable problems of improving teacher performance lie with the most experienced teacher: if this teacher cannot be changed by appraisal and target setting, then much of the investment purpose in an appraisal system is lost.

It is unadvisable to select only some staff for appraisal, however worthy the criteria appear. Clearly, selecting the sycophantic would lose the scheme its credibility, but so too would selecting only those thought to be weak or only those thought to be strong teachers. How demotivating to be selected as so weak and ineffective a teacher that an appraisal was thought to be the only cure? How much would other teachers strive to avoid being nominated as a candidate for the appraisal scheme? How could a scheme in such circumstances be used to develop others on the staff?

The same fears and reservations apply if only the most effective teachers are appraised. How can the weakest then be developed to an acceptable standard?

In short it would seem that all school staff, whatever their occupation, can be included in the appraisal process and that there are dangers for the scheme's credibility in omitting anyone. The lack of a plan to appraise the headteacher can also detract from the acceptability of a scheme; this key issue is discussed in Chapter 8.

WHO APPRAISES?

Appraisal is most commonly undertaken by a manager of a subordinate. In most primary schools with a staff of seven or less, appraisals commonly are undertaken by the headteacher. With increasing staff numbers, the control span becomes increasingly wide making it more difficult to have the necessary depth of knowledge of each teacher's work to conduct appraisals successfully. This cut-off point for an effective span of control may vary with factors such as:

The headteacher and his or her: experience as an appraiser; workload of other tasks; and knowledge of the staff.

The teachers and their: experience and competence in the basic task; confidence in being appraised; expectation of training and development.

The situation. Is it: a period of transition or of curriculum change? an induction for one or more teachers into the appraisal process? a new team of teachers still in the process of creating their behavioural norms? or a period of great time pressure?

In any system the point may be reached when the appraising becomes less meaningful because the appraiser is not sufficiently in touch with the work of the teacher. Appraisals then need to be delegated by the head to another senior member of staff who remains accountable to the headteacher. In a primary school a typical division might be that the head of the infant section appraises teachers in that department and the head of the school appraises the remainder of the staff. In a large junior school, the deputy head might manage appraisals of those who teach a particular age range, he or she appraised in turn by the headteacher. What is already, even in small schools, being developed is a form of organizational line management, a clear understanding of to whom each teacher is accountable. Looked at in another way, the system identifies who it is who helps, advises and manages the teacher and is responsible for his or her teaching performance. But in most secondary schools the question of who conducts the appraisal is much more complicated. The problem is illustrated by the case study of John Evans.

> John Evans is a Scale 2 teacher with special responsibility for visits and exchanges in the Modern Languages department of a large comprehensive school. He is a year tutor to a third year group and he trains and coaches the school third-year rugby team. In March last year he was scheduled to be responsible, in addition to teaching, preparing and marking for his language classes, for a school exchange with a school in Rouen, for the preparation of a set of 30 tutor reports on his group prior to their opting for their 4th year subjects, and for the planning and leading of a tour of South Wales with his school rugby squad.

> Under pressure from his Head of department, Mrs O'Brien, from his Head of year, Miss Barnard, and from the Head of Physical Education, Mr Rogers, John Evans felt in need of advice. He turned to the Deputy Headmistress Mrs Adams. 'They're all asking for my efforts at the same time,' he explained. 'None of them seems to understand the pressure I am under from the other two, and though the school year was well planned, no-one helps me plan my year. I don't want my teaching standard to fall, and I don't want to skimp any of the extra tasks I've been given. Please, Mrs Adams, whose demands take priority [Trethowan,1983]?'

Unless John Evans is helped to identify his appraiser, he may find himself accountable simultaneously to three or four people — a sure cause for conflict, stress and confused job aims. This problem of multiple accountability is best tackled by the line and project approach. This requires the nomination of one line manager for John Evans, who will appraise his work and with whom he will set targets. Any work undertaken by John Evans outside the department is appraised as a project by the person responsible for John's contribution and discussed with him and that appraisal fed back to John and his line manager as appraiser, who will most likely be the head of Languages Department. Feedback in John's case would come from the head of year and the head of Physical Education. If the workloads which John has undertaken come into conflict, John should discuss and resolve this with his head of department.

Since teachers have such strong affinity to their academic departments, it seems natural that their appraisers should be their departmental heads. This affinity is rooted in their academic discipline and their professional training and reinforced by the distribution of time in school. Most teachers feel they 'belong' to a particular department. For those few whose time is shared between departments, one departmental head should be nominated as the appraiser to whom any others would give feedback on the teacher's performance.

Only three groups within a staff do not easily fit into having a departmental head as line manager. These are: pastoral heads, whether of year or house; heads of departments themselves; and the deputy headteachers. Pastoral heads, whilst they teach in particular departments, may be seen to make their major contribution as leaders of pastoral units. As such they would be appraised and managed by a senior pastoral teacher or pastoral deputy head who would manage the implementation of the school's pastoral policy. The pastoral deputy receives feedback from the departmental head and others on the teaching performance of the senior pastoral team and incorporates this in the appraisal of their performance. Similarly, heads of departments would be appraised by a deputy headteacher, probably an academic deputy. The third group not managed by a departmental head would be the deputy headteachers themselves. Their line manager and appraiser is clearly the headteacher. The question of who appraises the headteacher is reserved for Chapters 8 and 9.

There is a place if not for appraisal of the appraiser by the subordinate then at least for feedback to the appraiser as it is the subordinate who receives the style the appraiser uses and who sees many of the strengths and weaknesses of the managerial performance. Relayed to the appraiser this feedback can help to improve and develop managerial performance. In most organizations appraisal 'by subordinates of those who manage them' does not extend beyond the level of feedback which the appraiser is free to accept or reject, to act on or to ignore. Probably any appraiser who to secure a good performance rating had only to impress his or her staff may not direct his or her decisions for the good of the organization but rather for the gratification of the staff. The appraiser's style would lack the task orientation of the McGregor's 'X manager' and be entirely in mould of the 'Y manager'. Subordinate feedback is an invaluable tool; subordinate appraisal is unlikely to produce an organizationally effective appraiser.

Much of what has been said about subordinate appraisal applies to peer appraisal. Several schools in Britain during 1983 and 1984 tried to introduce appraisal systems which would be 'friendly' to the user, popular with staff, impose little extra work or responsibility on the school hierarchy and not antagonize the teacher unions and associations. The result was peer appraisal.

An example of an embryo appraisal scheme which does not depend on being appraised by someone responsible for one's performance was the system set up at Queens' School, Bushey, in 1983. Headmaster Stan Bunnell lists some of its characteristics as:

> As the scheme was to be voluntary we would ourselves act as guinea pigs and also invite colleagues to volunteer.
>
> The 'appraiser' was to be the appraisee's choice from a panel which would, among others, include Heads of Department and Heads of House but need not necessarily be senior [Bunnell and Stephens, 1984].

It is however one of the prerequisites of all target setting and appraisal systems that each member of the staff of a school knows to whom he or she is accountable, with whom he or she will set targets and who appraises performance, and that the appraiser is responsible for the teacher's performance. Appraisal with responsibility is the only sure form of appraisal.

One chief fear of teachers before the general introduction of staff appraisal into schools has been the possibility of being assessed unfairly or incompetently by an appraiser. The best safeguards against this are two:

firstly the appropriate training of appraisers and secondly the opportunity for grandfather, leapfrog or second-tier interviews with the appraiser's appraiser. Who appraises the headteacher is dealt with in Chapter 8, but within any large school arrangement should be made for as many teachers as possible to have at least an option of a regular discussion with a member of staff who manages their appraiser's performance. For example, teachers who are appraised by their head of department should be invited to a leapfrog interview with the academic deputy. Heads of department who are appraised by a deputy headteacher should be given the option of an appraisal discussion with the head. In some schools this will be left as an optional 'safety valve' in the system to be taken up by those who wish to do so. In others it will be a more regular feature where all staff are expected to participate in a leapfrog interview (see Figure 5). Such an interview can:

- Compensate for a none too satisfactory interview at the lower level
- Add another perspective on the performance of all staff
- Assist with the early detection of grievances at the lower level
- Serve as a check on the appraisal system
- Serve for early detection of problems at the intermediate level
- Ensure equity between staff not only from different departments but even within the same department
- Ensure that the targets of teachers are coordinated throughout the school
- Serve as a means of control

Figure 5 Leapfrog interviews

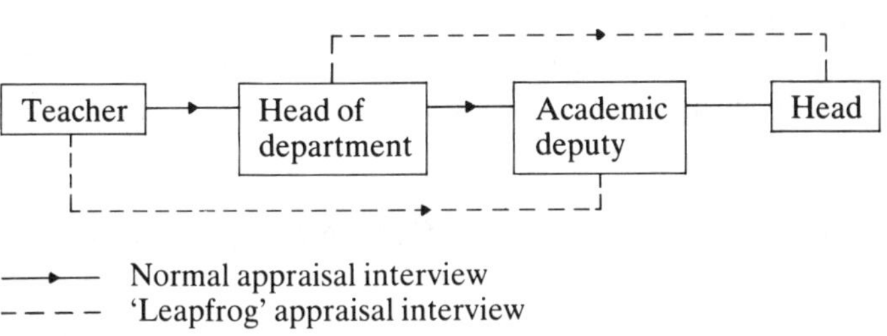

Its chief disadvantage is the amount of additional preparation and interview time which is added to the system, but there is too another disadvantage which may weaken the system unless it is well handled. This is the feeling given to the teacher that the appraisal by the head of department is of little importance compared with the later interview with the head of department's appraiser. Much of this feeling can be avoided by the manner and tone which the leapfrog interviewer uses in discussing the appraisal interview that took place between the teacher and head of department. 'You seem to have contributed well to your appraisal' or 'Your appraisal by your head of department looks to have been a very thorough one' or 'How are the targets you agreed with your head of department progessing?' Such comments convey implicitly that the leapfrog interview is not expecting to carry out appraisal afresh, but is willing to discuss or comment on an appraisal already completed and acted upon.

IS SELF-APPRAISAL USED?

The valuable contribution possible through self-appraisal and self-monitoring is discussed in Chapter 3. The designer of an appraisal system must consider to what extent self-appraisal will be used, and its importance to the overall final appraisal. The designer would omit all opportunity for self-appraisal with professionals such as teachers at his or her peril. Both commitment and development are encouraged by a participative approach, part of which is self-appraisal. Even widely differing schemes such as those set up at the Warden Park School, Cuckfield, and the Queens' School, Bushey, use self-appraisal. Warden Park distributes all its appraisal documents including the support checklist of major accountabilities to staff for their perception of their performance prior to interview. The Queens' School went even further, in allowing retrospective reappraisal.

'The agreed records would not be a dead or fixed statement or judgement but a reflection of on-going progress and could be destroyed, altered, added to after further discussion or consideration initiated by the appraisee' (Bunnell and Stephens, 1984). Few schools would advocate giving the teacher the power to alter or destroy an agreed record, but it is clear that the principle of using an element of self-appraisal in a teacher-appraisal system is an important one.

WHICH PERIOD OF PERFORMANCE IS TO BE APPRAISED?

There is a danger, when an appraisal interview is imminent, for an appraiser to gather recent evidence quickly on which to base an opinion on a performance. Recent performance however may not be typical and to be fair to the teacher an appraisal should reflect the whole appraisal period. For teachers the most usual appraisal period is the academic year since for the most part this is the period of a school timetable and of a constant programme of classes. However, if there are to be term or half-year interim reviews, the period to be appraised can be shortened to fit with the review dates. Some targets, too, will be completed well within the period of an academic year and can be reviewed at an agreed shorter interval.

WHAT IS TO BE THE MEASURE OF PERFORMANCE?

Within each system there must be methods of measuring what has been achieved. In some parts of the basic task or of targets set, the measures may be specific objective measures and in others professional subjective judgement may be the only measure possible. When objective criteria are used, they may still be subject to professional interpretation. The measures may be selected by the school or the LEA or they may be national measures. Whatever their source they must be agreed and understood by appraiser and teacher.

The measures for use with targets have already been discussed. The most common four are: time; finance, for example, spending within a budget; quantity; and quality.

Questions related to performance measures are:

Do both or only one of the parties measure the performance?

Are there to be interim measures to check that performance is on target?

If judgement is to be used will it be a pooled judgement by appraiser and teacher? If not can we specify whose judgement will count? If a third party's judgement is to be used this requirement should be agreed beforehand.

IS THERE TO BE AN APPRAISAL INTERVIEW?

An appraisal interview is an essential feature of professional appraisal. It is the main means of teacher contribution to an appraisal process. It presents the opportunity for guidance on career and on training and development needs and allows both parties to contribute to planning and target setting. Above all it is the occasion for listening to the teacher, to create an awareness of problems, underused talents and skills and constraints on performance. These general counselling, coaching and listening functions make an interview necessary. Only if the teacher were expected to accept a handed-down judgement would an interview not be essential. The appraisal of the teacher's performance would then be presented as a written statement and the teacher would sign in agreement. If however the appraisal judgement were to be rejected this would probably require a grievance interview to discuss the reasons for rejection. Clearly any professional teacher-appraisal scheme must contain provision for a one-to-one interview.

Factors in the planning of interviews have already been considered. In summary they are: timing in the school calendar; timing in relation to the interviews of other members of the department; timing and role of leapfrog interviews; location; and layout of the room.

IS THERE TO BE APPRAISAL DOCUMENTATION?

Although an appraisal can be conducted without any documentation at all, most systems develop documentation. Its purpose can be to:

- Create a written framework for the system and to guide people in its use
- Reflect development and changes in the system
- Indicate and summarize responsibilities and standards
- Define targets and their appraisal criteria
- Record achievements, decisions and aspirations

These main purposes of teacher-performance appraisal documentation can be achieved with five documents.

1. A description and explanation of the purposes and operation of the system
2. A document to encourage self-appraisal and to warm up the teacher to the themes which are open for discussion
3. A checklist of the principal accountabilities of the task, usually with space for a narrative or other appraisal of each
4. A target-setting sheet indicating the need for criteria, review dates and with space for an appraisal comment
5. Departmental review document

Documentation for appraisal is the subject of more detailed discussion in Chapter 6.

WHAT IS TO BE DONE ABOUT FUTURE PERFORMANCE?

An appraisal system whose main aim is performance improvement must clarify the ways in which it can be achieved. Normally there will be provision for a specific improvement target to be set and supported by counselling, developmental assignment and training with progress being reviewed at predetermined intervals. The concern may be for an improved performance in the present post or for preparation to fulfil a future post. Whatever the specific concern the nature and extent of the training and development available must be clear. Some possible forms of support are:

1. Self-development: reading; computer-assisted learning; tutor-directed learning; distance learning; audio/visual-course packages; and correspondence courses

2. On-the-job training: explain; demonstrate; provide an example; practice; coaching; and projects
3. Training courses: problem-identification group; problem-solving groups; brainstorming; in-tray exercise; case studies; structured activities; and role play or the like

A performance appraisal system which ends with the appraisal can still be demotivating and can defeat its own purpose unless it offers development opportunities. The appraisal and its interview are a means of identifying development and training needs. The gap that exists between present performance and desired future performance has to be filled through a development programme aiming to provide the teacher with the knowledge, skills and attitudes which will enable the performance to improve. However, it may be no easy task to identify which ingredient is missing in a performance or how training is to be given when that identification has been made. Under the question of future performance therefore there are two questions for consideration by the teacher and appraiser: What knowledge, skill or attitude is missing or deficient? and What form of development will best remedy this deficiency and so improve performance?

IS POTENTIAL TO BE RATED?

The proposal has been mooted on many occasions that a select group of potential high flyers within the profession should be identified in their early years of teaching and groomed for headship and other senior management posts in schools and within the education service generally. Whatever can be said about the equity, the ethics or the motivational effects of such a scheme, the greatest implementation problem of this proposal would be identifying the criteria to use to determine the high-flying group. Even if potential identification is not a scheme's main aim, those designing appraisal schemes may seek to use the information collected for the appraisal of performance, taking into account targets for future performance, to assess potential. The dangers of combining the various aims of appraisal schemes have already been discussed. Add to these the dangers brought by long-term grooming for future posts such as the self-fulfilling prophecy or the frustration of the teacher who has been promoted to the level of his or her own incompetence, but has yet to reach the forecast potential. The Peter Principle (Peter and Hull, 1969) with a promotion still to come!

Potential rating however should be distinguished from the unavoidable and justified consideration of a colleague's performance by a headteacher when selecting applicants for a promoted post. In that sense, almost inevitably a forecast or gamble is made at the time of appointment on a candidate's ability to fill a post he or she does not yet hold. A potential rating system is different in that it sets out in a systematic way to identify the potential of all teachers on a regularly reviewed procedure, mainly for future long-term career goals.

The data needed to help with such judgements should, if used at all, be drawn together into the appraisal system so that the best available information is used. The chief sources of such information are: the teacher's own career goal; the teacher's own self-appraisal of potential; the appraiser's assessment of the teacher's potential; observation by advisers and senior education staff, but probably not by course leaders; and tests.

The teacher's own career goal

Consideration should be given when assessing potential for senior promoted posts to the teacher's own interest in promotion. Some may have the ability to hold a particular type of post but not want to do so. For some teachers promotion benefits have to be balanced against those of a pattern of living and working associated with the present post. Other teachers feel that the responsibility of promotion is not adequately rewarded and do not seek promotion for that reason. On the other hand, some teachers may have a career goal which in the view of the appraiser is unrealistically high. Generally, however, most teachers' career goals are pitched within their ability and the well-designed potential appraisal system will solicit and incorporate this information.

The teacher's own self-appraisal of potential

The weaknesses of self-appraisal have been reviewed earlier, and the system which wishes to appraise potential should bear these in mind. However, just as there is much to be learned in performance appraisal from the teacher's self-assessment, so there is in potential appraisal. The appraiser can for example so easily mistake quietness for shyness or lack of confidence. Lack of opportunity to lead or to administer can be interpreted as lack of confidence in that direction. Self-appraisal of potential can give enough of an indication of latent ability to correct an appraiser's ill-formed opinion.

The appraiser's assessment of the teacher's potential

The appraiser may have a sound assessment of the teacher's present performance from working with him or her and from observation. Potential assessment is much more difficult. The promoted post may require qualities not needed or used in the teaching post. Many qualities of a good chief education officer, such as negotiating skills, leadership or the 'helicopter' mind that absorbs a wide general field, are given less reign in the teaching situation. Such qualities may easily be missed by an appraiser intent on assessing present teaching performance, especially if the teaching performance is not particularly good. Yet frequently the lack of success in a post does not mean that the teacher could not successfully hold a higher level position which used his or her greater strengths. A further complicating factor is the appraiser's assessing potential beyond his or her own experience, understanding and ability.

Observation by advisers and senior education staff

Though there is no particular reason why someone senior to the teacher and the appraiser should have any more success in identifying potential it may be useful to draw into the appraisal process those who already hold posts to which the teacher aspires. A teacher who feels, along with the appraiser, that he or she could be an effective adviser may have that opinion confirmed by working or talking with a member of the advisory staff. Though such 'outside' appraisal of potential is insufficient in itself it can make a useful contribution to the process.

One group who may also have useful views are those who lead or teach on development courses for teachers. However, there are dangers for the course leader in this being set up as a formal process, in the effect it has on the trust which is necessary between course leader and teacher. It can also affect not only the individual's performance on the course but the relationship between course participants and the course ethos in general.

Tests

Some industrial companies attempting to identify potential send staff on assessment courses to undertake a variety of tests. Few such tests at present available seem relevant to the leadership of schools. However, more simple and practical role play, simulation and in-tray exercises can be means of identifying potential. Appraisal-system designers will be aware however that an ability to role play successfully is no firm guarantee that the teacher can perform as effectively in real life.

Another inexpensive test form is the interview, usually reserved for those identified as possible high flyers. An interview board would be the responsibility of an LEA rather than an individual school. The increased use of internal appointments within LEAs in recent years may make this practice a more useful one which could contribute to the development of a uniform approach to management and management development.

A final consideration is how much of the appraisal of potential is conveyed to the teacher. Doubtless, in all other appraisal aspects the teacher *should have* full knowledge of all information, evidence and related decisions. Are there other considerations when assessing potential? How frustrating is it to know that one has the potential to be promoted to headship but that such promotion is unavailable? What effect does it have on the head of a school to know that the head of geography department is a potentially outstanding headteacher in the opinion of the LEA? What effect would such knowledge have on that geographer's colleagues at school? Potential appraisal clearly brings associated problems and, although it offers some benefits, should be incorporated within an appraisal system only with the greatest of care, if at all. It should never be combined with a performance-improvement appraisal system.

WHAT IS THE RELATIONSHIP OF SALARY TO APPRAISAL?

The risks in relating salary for the forthcoming year to the appraisal of performance of the previous year have already been discussed. It seems unlikely that the whole of a teacher's salary will be decided by this method, but the Secretary of State for Education and Science and others have, from time to time, suggested various additions to salary for good performance.

The implications for system design for a salary-related system are concerned firstly with making the best decision possible on the quality of performance. The appraiser is unlikely to make the decision on who secures which salary addition and it is much more probable that the appraiser will pass a ranking of staff performance to a central source such as the LEA central offices for moderation. If, however, merit additions are to be awarded by the school, an allocation system of merit additions to each school has to be devised. This may be based upon criteria such as:

- Size of school (i.e., numbers of staff or of pupils)
- Success in achieving certain LEA approved school targets (e.g., examination results, introduction of approved courses, etc.)
- Degree of difficulty of the teaching task in the catchment area (e.g., many ethnic minority groups, educational priority area, etc.)

Another design implication for a system which strongly links performance and salary is the rating of performances so that comparison can be made with other performances in the school. A decision may be needed on who awards these grades, who moderates the various judgements, and who provides the information to the appraiser to help in making the judgement on grading. This grading and moderation would be most difficult to achieve within schools.

A more realistic use for the salary addition is as an incentive to a teacher to accept a particular major target which the school would like to see achieved. This runs close to the project system of staff development and is an effective means of using additions to salary. Its chief risk is the precedent it may set for staff who feel a merit addition should be automatic on accepting any school target.

HOW OFTEN DO APPRAISALS TAKE PLACE?

Most school-appraisal systems are based upon the academic year with targets set for the beginning of the year in September and appraised at the end in July. There may be interim reviews at mid-year or termly. The Warden Park system, for example, has its targets set in July ready for the following September and the review of performance in June, except for those related to external examination results which are appraised in September. In that system the interims are a leapfrog interview in the autumn term with the headmaster and an interim review in the spring term with the teacher's appraiser.

The key questions on timing are: What is to be the interval between appraisal interviews? Will it be a fixed period or will it vary with target or performance being appraised? Will there be interim reviews? (If so, the occasion for these should be agreed.) Is there to be a leapfrog interview? If so, will this be as a matter of course or will it serve as the system of appeal?

Whatever the system timing is agreed to be, only exceptional circumstances should cause that to be changed. The unexpected surprise appraisal may be fine for the megalomanic appraiser, but it destroys confidence and trust in the unfortunate teacher.

HOW IS FAIRNESS MAINTAINED BETWEEN TEACHERS?

Fairness is the basis of trust and respect between appraiser and teacher. In the appraisal interview they discuss and negotiate an appraisal with which both are happy and the usual method of ensuring that the teacher is content with an appraisal is to ask him or her to sign the form to that effect. When the teacher has some reservations he or she comments to that effect on the form.

It is also usual for the appraiser's decision to carry in the event of a disagreement, which implies the power of the appraiser to accept the teacher's version. In the event of a deadlocked appraisal, referral would be made on the leapfrog system to the appraiser's appraiser. System designers might consider adding a further referee such as the chairman of governors or an LEA adviser. This referral system can include the statutory grievance procedure. If it does not, then that procedure must be made explicit as a route to which any teacher has recourse.

IS ANY APPRAISAL INFORMATION USED CENTRALLY?

Most school-appraisal systems, even if designed to meet local or national criteria will be operated within the organization of a single school. In most cases all information generated will remain within the school, if only because of the overwhelming volume of paper that would accumulate at the LEA administrative centre. Many targets, appraisals and other information generated will be virtually meaningless outside the particular school. For these reasons most schemes are designed to give copies only to the teacher, appraiser and head with whom all information remains confidential. Some schemes however extend their confidentiality to allow certain extracts from the collected appraisal information to be pooled for use by the LEA.

The most obvious item of collected information for the LEA from its school teacher-appraisal system would be the training and development needs of its teachers. By far the greater part of this training and development will be undertaken within the schools themselves but the LEA training-and-development officer will need to be aware of this. However, that part of the training need which will be provided at a central source must be analyzed. The need may most cost-effectively be met by methods such as: courses; lectures and films; interpersonal-skills training; problem-identifying and -solving groups; and group learning.

Centrally provided group training meets needs beyond those of the individual or the school. Group training draws together all those teachers from various schools who have a common training need. It allows those people to discuss, support and advise each other in a way which no individual training can provide. It allows the LEA through its staff trainers to meet the needs of as many people as possible and to spread new ideas to a wide audience. Linked with a cascade system of training it becomes the most cost-effective method of supporting an appraisal system and of improving performance.

This does not eliminate the possibility of provider-initiated courses or of LEA initiated meetings to raise the level of awareness in certain fields. But it does shift the emphasis of in-service training from provider initiation to purchaser initiation (LEA) and to user initiation (schools). The designer of the appraisal system should consider to what extent this important aspect of appraisal systems is to be used and build into the scheme an analysis of training and development needs.

In addition, feedback on the efficacy of training can be obtained over a long period. Appraisal, by the participant, of a course of training immediately upon its completion, is probably standard practice and if not it most certainly should be. Longer term feedback is much more difficult to obtain. Yet, with an appraisal system, a training need which was identified and was met by a external group-training procedure can be more accurately evaluated many months later. Did the interviewing skills learned on a staff-selection course prove useful in practice back at school? Were the new techniques, for example, to teach spelling, better with the pupils than those already in use? If the problems which led to the group-training activity being offered are still remaining long after the course is completed, then honest, regular feedback will help the provider to evaluate, reexamine and redesign the activity to improve its usefulness.

Whether any other appraisal information should be centrally pooled is a matter to be considered by the system designer. Other information which might be considered, although not always recommended, for central use is:

- Assessment of teacher potential
- Poor performers — teachers whose performance in the basic task is causing concern
- Outstanding performers — teachers who have successfully completed major projects for the school whether or not these projects carried a 'merit' addition to salary
- Teacher age, skill, experience, mobility and the like allow an LEA to build a skills-and-experience audit and to facilitate teacher forecasting and possibly succession planning

Finally, it cannot be stressed too strongly that any information which is pooled centrally either must be anonymous (e.g., the percentage of graduate men and women per school staff) or there must be a clear declaration to the teachers beforehand of which items of appraisal information will remain confidential to named individuals within school and which will be passed on to the central information system of the LEA.

HOW CONFIDENTIAL IS THE INFORMATION?

The success of an appraisal interview depends largely upon the trust which exists between teacher and appraiser. The performance discussion must be 'full and frank' with the participants free to identify weaknesses and reveal feelings. In these circumstances teacher or appraiser may well reveal information which neither would want passed on to others. The basic rule therefore for an appraisal system is participant control of the information. The teacher who exposes to the appraiser that his or her class control is much weaker than is generally appreciated or who has a continuing family tragedy which will adversely affect teaching performance in the next few months may well not want this information passed on to others. Why would anyone reveal information which will be recorded, centrally pooled with the LEA and maybe used later to jeopardize a promotion? Therefore the first rule of confidentiality must be that information revealed verbally in an appraisal interview remains confidential to the interview participants.

However, for most appraisal systems the confidentiality of the written information on the appraisal documents is a little wider. Such information remains confidential to: the teacher; the appraiser; the appraiser's appraiser (which in most schools will be the headteacher); and the headteacher. To these can be added the LEA. If it is, then it may be decided to name the post of the LEA officers to whom it may be revealed. Alternatively, it may be agreed that only certain items of the written appraisal information will be passed on to the LEA, once again with or without nominating the post of those to have access. Whatever is agreed, this undertaking should be clearly written into the appraisal-system description; made known to all parties; and strictly adhered to. The disposal of one appraisal document should be the decision of the teacher. This is the warm-up document, completed by the teacher prior to the appraisal interview. The disposal possibilities have already been discussed and in summary they are: retained by the teacher after being used as an interview 'crib sheet'; or given to the appraiser to form part of the appraisal record, being then subject to the same rules of confidentiality as other written appraisal information

Finally, any private notes made by either party to an appraisal interview remain confidential and under the same rules as verbal comments made for that interview.

ARE THERE OTHER USES FOR THE APPRAISAL INFORMATION?

Most uses of the appraisal information have already been identified and discussed, but three further uses need to be clarified. First, appraisal information can be of use in staff and succession planning within the school. The possibility of staffing information being used centrally by the LEA has been discussed, but within the school it will facilitate short-term planning to be aware of the career ambitions, development experience and training of the staff. It should be of little surprise to the school senior management to see staff applications for particular internal or external posts or to see which teachers are *not* making applications, though apparently well qualified to do so. It should be clear who has been or is being trained through delegation for a specific school task and to whom one may turn when seeking a temporary stand-in for a post, duty or task. To have this information available the top management of the school has to extract appropriate information from the appraisal documents and then coordinate, collate and retrieve it.

If the preceding use of appraisal information illustrated the need for extracted and collated information, a second of the many spin-off uses for appraisal documents shows the need for a copy of the targets to be readily available to appraiser and teacher. This is for use as a day-to-day reminder of the targets set. If targets are to be achieved they should be reread from time to time and compared with present behaviour. If what is being done conflicts with the target, or if nothing much is being done towards target achievement, this handy reminder will put the teacher back on course.

A third use for appraisal information illustrates the need for a copy of the annual sets of records to be retained with the headteacher or whoever writes the official reference within the school.

References are frequently required in a hurry and it is sometimes difficult to do justice to a colleague's past performance and to be guided instead only by recent events. An appraisal record will show not only performance in the basic task but number, complexity and difficulty of the targets which have been undertaken over the years and the degree of success achieved. Whilst this is clearly not all that is called for in a reference on a colleague, the appraisal documents will record many features of past performance on which a reference or testimonial may be based.

To summarize, the chief guideline when designing an appraisal system is to identify its aim and produce appropriate organization and documentation to achieve it. However, bear in mind the many other uses of appraisal information if given to the right people at the right time and appropriately collated.

Ask most teachers the who, what, when, where and how of the appraisal system with which they would be happy to work and their replies would not be too dissimilar from these:

Who? A person in whom I have confidence, whose expertise I respect and to whom I am accountable

What? I expect an appraisal to relate to my job description and any special targets I have. I expect to negotiate the criteria and have them clearly stated

When? Over a negotiated but stated period and not based upon an isolated or hasty judgement

Where? Throughout the school day but ending each appraisal period with a free discussion with a formal conclusion

Why? To let me know how I am doing and to help me develop personally and professionally so that I can become a better teacher and can achieve my potential

How? School-based, in a professional way, as described, and with a written concluding statement.

6 DOCUMENTATION

'Tis hard to say, if greater want of skill
Appear in writing or in judging ill.

Alexander Pope, *Essay on Criticism*

Appraisal is essential to management but appraisal forms are not essential to appraisal. If written evidence is needed to support an appraisal or to record its agreements then prose statements on an A4 sheet will serve the purpose. Appraisal documentation will probably develop with the system, but it will be little more than an orderly *aide-mémoire* of aspects of appraisal that the participants should be sure to consider. So, if documents are to be produced it must be remembered that they are there to help the appraisal along and not to create a barrier between teacher and appraiser.

The documentation of a system must reflect its purpose. Trite as it may seem, it is with surprising frequency that the documents used in one established scheme are transferred into a newly created one, without sufficient attention to matching it with the scheme aims. However, it may be useful to examine other appraisal documents to stimulate creativity in designing for a new system.

KEY DOCUMENTS IN AN APPRAISAL SYSTEM

The main documents needed in an appraisal system are:

1. An explanation of the system including its: purpose; personnel; and practices
2. A self-appraisal document (the warm-up document) covering: career plan; negative features of the past year; positive features of the past year; and general comment on any relevant subject which the teacher wishes to raise
3. A statement of the principal accountabilities of the basic task and space for their appraisal. If required this document may include: performance

grading list; space for particular strengths and weaknesses revealed in the teacher in working to achieve the task; space for action plan to improve future performance; space for additional accomplishments not reflected in the basic task but related to it; space for the teacher's comments; space for a leapfrog or second-level comment; and space for signatures of the participants

4. A target document which includes: space for the targets set for the forthcoming year together with their essential performance criteria; space to comment on target review and achievement; and space for participant signatures, unless this document is combined with the previous document

5. Departmental review document to cover topics such as: syllabuses; room-and-space allocation; departmental organization; finance; staffing; examination results; achievements; targets; and space for comment on target review and achievements

This review should cover the past year, the forthcoming year and the long-term future of up to five years ahead.

Several of the five basic documents can be combined in their presentation. The explanation of the system, for example, can be attached to the warm-up document or to the statement of principal accountabilities. Whether or not it is included in another document, that explanation must appear very early in the appraisal cycle. Other possibilities for combined documents are the principal accountabilities and the target-setting sheets, as these documents will almost always be used on the same occasions and will apply to all staff. An effective combination of documents therefore would be:

Document A: Explanation of the system combined with the self-awareness document

Document B: Principal accountabilities of the basic task combined with the target document

Document C: Departmental review document

None should prove to be too bulky, and none should exceed four sides of A4 paper. Many organizations use different colours for each of their documents for ease of identification. Using the above combination of documents, let us examine in detail the design, content and layout of each on a folded A2 (i.e. double A4) sheet.

DOCUMENT A: EXPLANATION OF THE SYSTEM COMBINED WITH THE AWARENESS DOCUMENT

Since personal, subjective information should not be presented on the outside of a document that space should be reserved for an explanation of the system. The tone of this explanation, which is the teacher's first contact with the appraisal documentation should be clear, succinct and friendly. After the title of the scheme and document, there should be a space for the teacher's name and for some other identification information on the outside of the document. Next should come the description of the purpose of the scheme and the instructions on the use of this particular document. A specimen Document A is shown at the end of this chaper.

Inside the performance-awareness document will be items to stimulate a form of self-appraisal, the three main aspects of which are career proposals, performance in the year gone by and general factors related to performance. It may be helpful to make the teacher distinguish between long- and short-term career goals, but in general too many questions in this section may appear to be placing too high a premium on a desire for promotion. Also, unless any questions on career are carefully phrased, there is the possibility of appearing to be pressing the teacher along a predetermined path.

In the second section devoted to the past year, the main subdivision can be between its negative and positive features. The positive are necessary to:

- Make the teacher aware that there are enjoyable and rewarding features which may be in danger of being overlooked
- Ensure that the appraiser is aware of the achievements of the teacher
- Ensure that the appraiser is aware of the work interests of the teacher
- Remind the appraiser of the forms of support which the teacher has valued during the year, for example, courses, help from colleagues, and projects

Also in this second section it is important to encourage the teacher to face up to any negative aspects of the year's performance. Questions which ask about such matters confirm the interest of the school in total performance, not only in its successful items. Any questions which search out disappointments, unpleasant tasks, frustrations, a sense of waste, the lack of certain skills encourage both appraiser and teacher to see the performance as it really is. As the teacher is being asked to be thoroughly frank, then he or she must retain control of this document and pass it into the formal appraisal system containing only those written remarks with which he or she is at ease. The discussion, however, must be open and participative and the document can do much to stimulate such discussion by its range of questioning.

The final section of the self-appraisal document seeks to offer the teacher the opportunity to raise any matter at all which has a bearing on performance. In the provided example of this document little guidance is given in the final section except to encourage the teacher to comment on the school and on the appraisal scheme as a whole. The document thus progresses from matters affecting the individual (e.g., career goals) to those affecting the whole organization.

DOCUMENT B: PRINCIPAL ACCOUNTABILITIES OF THE BASIC TASK COMBINED WITH THE TARGET DOCUMENT

Document B, sometimes called the *task-and-target document*, lays out what each teacher is expected to achieve during the year. It is prepared in June ready to come into operation at the beginning of the first term in the academic year in September.

As with Document A, its front page should not contain confidential information, but it can usefully be divided into three sections. The first section would contain general information on the teacher — name, post, scale, department. The second could remind the users of the procedures in this part of the appraisal system. The third could contain the basic-task checklist, described earlier, which outlines the teacher's principal accountabilities and as such applies to all teachers in the school.

On page 2 of the task-and-target sheet the same checklist can be repeated, but with the principal headings only, leaving plenty of space for a description of or a comment upon the teacher's performance in each of the named areas. Since sometimes there is, on the part of the teacher, a significant accomplishment which is not part of the basic task and was not nominated a target at the beginning of the year, it may be prudent to leave space at the bottom of page 2 for Additional Accomplishments. For example, a teacher has helped a colleague significantly through a difficult term or perhaps devised a new procedure which will now be developed for general school use. This or a range of other achievements can be recorded and the teacher thus be given credit and thanked.

Page 3 lists the targets set with the teacher for the year just ended. At the beginning of the year these were agreed and recorded on this document. It is important to remind the document users here that 'if performance of the basic task is unsatisfactory, any target set must include a target which aims to strengthen the unsatisfactory area'. The need to be explicit in target setting and to identify performance criteria, target priority and completion date is stressed earlier. The appraisal-document design must reflect this importance and make it difficult for the users to omit or forget to set vital target information. Additional sheets should be available if necessary to allow for a full description of targets and their criteria.

An optional section, depending upon the requirements of the system, can be added to page 3. This is an opportunity to appraise performance overall. This can be done through behaviour descriptions as in the example overleaf, or by giving some form of numbered gradings. There is no particular necessity to grade performances unless this information is needed for salary purposes. 'Ticks in boxes' and 'grading of performance' are unpopular features of appraisal systems. System designers are advised against their use unless such features are a necessary facet of the scheme. The basic division needed in performance appraisal is between the teacher who met or exceeded the standards required and those who need attention and support to be able to meet them. However, in the example given at the end of this chapter a third and higher category has been created to indicate superior achievements and if it is felt that this recognition could be a useful feature of the system, then the task-and-target document must be so designed.

Page 4 does two things. It ensures that the participants are clear on which areas of performance need to be strengthened, since this most important information may form the basis of one of the targets set for the teacher in the year ahead. Precision here will make the setting of that target all the easier. The second feature of this last page is the provision for agreement and comment. Appraiser and teacher should sign the form, and there should be space for the teacher to comment on the appraisal. Finally, the document needs space for provision of a second-level or leapfrog interview and for reviewer's comments.

DOCUMENT C: DEPARTMENTAL REVIEW DOCUMENT

Departmental review is an aspect of appraisal which need not necessarily form part of performance appraisal. It is possible to confine appraisal to the performance of individual teachers, yet since teachers all work within the departments it is often appropriate to develop team appraisal and to use it with departmental teams.

A document which sets out to appraise departments needs three sections, one devoted to each of last year, next year and the long-term future. Section 1 should look at the year which is ending and review the department's problems and achievements. A suggested Document C model is given at the end of this chapter. Most reviews would include topics such as: the current strengths and weaknesses of the department; the syllabus; organizational problems; departmental meetings; records of work, and the like; staffing; staff courses; major departmental achievements; outstanding members of the department this year; examination results; and department targets achieved.

The second section would cover similar topics but in relation to the forthcoming year.

The third section should encourage a department to look at the long-term future and assess over a five-year period the likely problems and targets in syllabus design, examinations, staffing, departmental organization, finance, rooms and space.

Clearly Document C is in the form of a prompt list. As such it forms the basis of a discussion between the head and the head of department. The list neither exhaustive nor prescriptive is likely to direct the thinking of the department along lines which the school requires. A nice balance is struck between open appraisal, for which there is no documentation required other than a blank sheet and the directed appraisal which prescribes in the detail how the department will be assessed.

OTHER ASPECTS OF DOCUMENTATION

In the earlier examination of appraisal documentation, the basic-task appraisal took the form of narrative appraisal against a checklist of principal accountabilities. Performance was expected to be extended in almost every case with up to six targets each with its own performance criteria.

This combination is a sufficient appraisal to achieve at least an operating minimum performance and to provide the possibility of professional development through targets. Such targets can be high but achievable and set by the mature and well-motivated teacher or, at the other extreme, targets imposed by the school on a teacher who lacks the ability or the willingness to achieve the basic task.

GRADING PERFORMANCE

Unless the system is related to salary or promotion, there is no sound reason in performance appraisal for a grading on performance. However, if a grading is necessary, it is possible using only the two facets of performance previously discussed (basic task and targets) to combine these into rating categories. The simplest categorization is clearly into those teachers who achieved what was set and those who did not. This is not too difficult for a standard basic task but with individually set targets this clearly raises the problem of a teacher who engineers to have easily achievable targets and with little effort achieves them, being compared with the teacher who accepts difficult targets, makes greater efforts but only barely achieves them. In any nonstandard performance allowance must always be made for the difficulty of the task being achieved. Bearing this in mind the simplest grading of overall performance might resemble Figure 6.

Figure 6 Performance grading — four grades

Got the job done by achieving all target-and-task requirements and by exceeding some		Needed on-going direction and guidance	
Overall performance met high standards set for teachers at this school		Did not get the job done	
(Tick the appropriate box)			

It would be reasonable to increase the satisfactory gradings of performance further and thus cater for the identification of superior achievements. Thus, the overall performance would comprise: considering task performance, target achievement and any additional accomplishments, selecting the statement in Figure 7 which most accurately describes the teacher's overall performance in the past year.

Figure 7 Performance grading — six grades

Superior achievements		Met or exceeded high goals		Needs attention	
Performance clearly surpassed expectations and substantially affected the school or department. The teacher markedly improved prior practices and/or developed new approaches		Got the job done by achieving all targets and requirements and by exceeding some		Needed on-going direction and guidance	
Performance clearly surpassed expectations for all target-and-task requirements. The teacher improved prior practices and/or developed new approaches		Overall performance met the high standards set for teachers at this school		Did not get the job done	
(Tick the appropriate box)					

PASS/FAIL CONCEPT

Another possible form of appraisal, frequently used in the late 1970s in the Eastern Seaboard states of the USA, was the use of a checklist against a pass/fail concept. Discussing this with teachers at the time, it appeared that they felt it met a legal requirement to appraise teachers but did little to motivate through the recognition of good or outstanding performance. Those teachers who were not unsatisfactory were by definition satisfactory. This category covered all manner of performances from the not very willing and the not very able who scarcely made the grade to the most able, mature and willing teacher on the staff. However, in that system a final page was later added which required, under the heading of Recommendations, the recording of all forms of improvement required in borderline performances. Under Commendations, outstanding performances or aspects of performances were recognized. Document D illustrating this approach is included at the end of this chapter.

In another USA school district in the late 1970s a five-point scale was being used to rate teacher (or in this particular case, counsellor) performance. The five gradings had the following significance:

> 5 = Outstanding. (Counsellor exhibits this quality to a very high degree; very rare that this would occur more than a few times in a total evaluation.)
> 4 = An area of definite strength for counsellor.
> 3 = Meets all the expectations of a counsellor in this school district.
> 2 = Area that needs some improvement.
> 1 = Area that needs considerable improvement. (Counsellor exhibits serious deficiencies which need immediate improvement.)
>
> In addition to the five ratings above a + or - may be used at any time to indicate progress or lack of progress in a specific area.

The evaluation would be undertaken by two of the staff together with a self-appraisal and the resulting appraisals would form the bases of a narrative report and targets (or 'goals') for the counsellor for the year ahead. The actual instructions read:

> It is intended that the evaluation form would be completed separately by the counsellor, the principal and the department head. Sometime in August, all three would get together to go over the completed form and to discuss any areas of disagreement or concern. Goals would be established for the coming year and an anecdotal report written, using the evaluation form as the basis for both. Sometime in February or March, principal, counselor and department head would get together to discuss briefly progress made towards agreed upon goals.

Document E illustrating this approach is included at the end of this chapter.

The school in the USA which used this appraisal appeared to have good working relationships and saw no problems in producing a narrative report on a counsellor which perhaps stated that all three assessors of a performance rated its quality differently. 'We just sit right down and discuss it,' said the counsellor concerned.

BEHAVIOURALLY ANCHORED RATING SCALES

An approach to appraisal which attempts to reduce the amounts of subjectivity in the process is the construction of behaviourally anchored rating scales. At present no such rating scales exist which are widely used in teacher appraisal, although the new form of staff appraisal recommended to the Metropolitan Police Force in 1985 attempts to use a set of such scales. However, the construction and validation of behaviourally anchored rating scales are an expensive and time-consuming process.

The construction of such a scale for teachers begins with the researchers asking teachers to describe effective and ineffective teaching behaviour in a large number of critical incidents. This requires teachers to lay aside the frequent comment of appraisers of teacher behaviour: 'I can't describe it but I know it when I see it.' The researchers must be given the specific descriptions of behaviour in certain situations and the sufficient descriptions to create not only the extremes but up to 10 intermediate categories of behaviour. When aggregated, these specific observable behaviours are intended equal total job performance.

Apart from expense and time in construction these rating scales continue to present operating problems:

- They are still subject to the middle-grade syndrome. Appraisers steer away from superlatives leaving an inordinately high percentage of appraisees in middle grades of performance.
- They are still subject to the 'horns' and 'halo' effects, that is, tendency for an appraiser to be influenced by past good or bad appraisals, rather than by the current year's performance.
- They tend, in practice, not to be as universally applicable as it might be hoped. Appropriate behaviour in a teacher may still be judged differently according to area or even school. In fact, it could well be argued that appropriate teacher behaviour must necessarily vary with location and with other factors. If this is so, an 'excellent' teacher performance in one area may not be excellent in another.
- Occasionally, in the construction of these scales, certain essential skills and qualities may have to be omitted because the researchers find it impossible to break them down into observable behaviours and so to assess

them. Examples are the quality of having a pleasing voice and the strangely unassessable yet important quality of 'integrity'. If there are several such examples of essential skills, behaviours and qualities being omitted, the rating scale tends to present a distorted representation of the post and thereby a distorted appraisal.

The greatest potential advantages from behaviourally anchored rating scales are firstly that the scale can be linked to actual job requirements rather than abstract qualities. Secondly, because it depends upon observation rather than upon subjective judgement it can reduce appraisal error. However, before such a rating scale could be included in teacher-appraisal documentation, it would need wide research in its construction and testing to satisfy teachers and appraisers that the tool was achieving its purpose.

SAMPLE DOCUMENTS

The documents in this section illustrate discussions earlier in the chapter. Documents A, B and C represent those likely to be found in the UK in the Wessex County Council Teacher Development Scheme. Documents D and E illustrate USA appraisal forms in the Nonsuch School District.

DOCUMENT A: PERFORMANCE AWARENESS AND SELF-APPRAISAL

Teacher's name:		Post and scale:
School	Department	Date planned for this appraisal:

PURPOSE

The purpose of this appraisal scheme is to develop teachers and improve the quality of their performance so that we can provide for pupils the highest possible standards of education.

PROCEDURES

We aim to achieve our purpose by:

1. Reviewing performance of each teacher in his or her present post over the past year.
2. Establishing both the achievements and the underachievements.
3. Preparing a clear achievable performance plan for the year ahead.

An appraisal review is an annual event between an appraiser and an individual teacher. To be most effective the appraisal discussion must be open and participative. Appraisals should also improve the working relationship between the teacher and the appraiser through clearer joint views of performance and targets. To achieve this, teacher and appraiser must:

FIRSTLY

Arrange to meet during June. When the meeting is fixed the appraiser should give the teacher a blank copy of this performance awareness and self-appraisal document. The teacher already has a copy from last year of the task-and-target document. Teachers should complete the performance awareness and self-appraisal sheet as far as they feel able to do so, and bring it to the review meeting which has been agreed.

SECONDLY

The appraiser should use his or her copy of the teacher's task-and-target document to note the areas where the teacher performs well or badly. In making this professional judgement use any notes, observations or the like to ensure that the whole year is being appraised and not merely recent performance.

THIRDLY

In the meeting:

1. Review the past year using the task-and-target document. Agree to what extent performance has been sound and targets have been achieved. Please be sure that the teacher understands how much the school appreciates all positive contributions to the department. If there is a performance area which needs development the teacher should agree with the appraiser whether any help will be requested in securing an improvement.
2. Review the points the teacher wants to raise from the performance awareness and self-appraisal document.
3. Agree upon targets for the teacher to achieve during the next academic year. Record these on a new task-and-target sheet and agree their criteria and priority. Discuss resources which may be needed to help in target achievement and how they will be allocated.
4. Send the new task-and-target sheet for typing and, after checking, for distribution to the head, the appraiser and the teacher.
5. Thank you for your cooperation. Feel free to discuss with the headteacher any problems which are not resolved with the head of department.

1. Overall Career Plan

(i) What are your short- and long-term career plans?

Short Term:

Long Term:

(ii) Is there any special coaching you would like from anyone on the staff?

2. Review of the Past Year

A. The positive aspect of the past 12 months

(i) What kinds of work experiences have given you the greatest satisfaction over the past year?

(ii) Have any classes or pupils been particularly rewarding?

(iii) Has anyone in particular on the staff been of special help this year?

(iv) Which forms of training or courses of further education have you undertaken this year? (Remember to consider departmental training within your department or house as well as external courses.)

B. The negative aspect of the past 12 months

(i) What do you dislike doing that you must do in your present job?
(ii) Have any tasks been especially difficult this year?
(iii) Have any classes or pupils not been satisfactorily dealt with?
(iv) Which of your skills and talents are most underused?
(v) What aspects need strengthening of your technical competence, managerial competence, personal relationships, etc.?
(vi) Would you wish to attend courses on these? Or how else do you propose to gain the necessary experience and improvement?

3. General

(i) Do you have any positive comments to make about the school?
(ii) Do you have any suggestions for improving the school?
(iii) Are there any general comments you wish to make about any matter affecting you?
(iv) Do you have an up-to-date job description? Do you feel that you understand all the requirements of your task?
(v) Are you satisfied with the opportunities you have to discuss your problems, your targets and your work in general?

DOCUMENT B:
TASKS AND TARGETS September 198__ to July 198__

<table>
<tr><td colspan="3">Teacher's name:</td><td colspan="2">Post and scale:</td></tr>
<tr><td>School:</td><td>Department:</td><td colspan="2">Duties of scale point outside department</td><td>Years at school</td></tr>
<tr><td>Appraiser's name:</td><td>Post and scale:</td><td>Date of this appraisal</td><td colspan="2">Date of previous appraisal</td></tr>
</table>

PROCEDURES

1. *At the beginning of the appraisal period*, the appraiser and the teacher clarify, discuss jointly, develop targets and performance measures for the appraisal period, using last year's task-and-target appraisal document.
2. *During the appraisal period*, significant changes in targets are discussed between appraiser and teacher and amended on this task-and-target document.
3. *At the end of the appraisal period*, the results are discussed with the teacher. Unsolved problems should be discussed with the headteacher.

After the head, teacher and appraiser have signed the appraisal, the head forwards the original for typing and distribution to the teacher, the appraiser and the head (in teacher's file).

Area	Description of performance
1. Pastoral	Knowledge of every child as an individual acting *in loco parentis* Running tutor group to create a group relationship Carrying out tutor programme obligatory activities Reporting to parents Contributing to development as a tutor Contributing to effective house organization Identification of problems of tutor group members
2. Teaching	Preparation of lessons Classroom management including safety of pupils Marking of class and homework Evaluation of pupils' achievements, awareness of their abilities, problems and personalities
3. Personal skills development	Subject related skills Professional skills development Development of others Deputizing and sharing responsibility Motivation of pupils
4. Departmental and school community	Participation in extracurricular activities Contribution to morale Development of professional attitude, appearance, conduct Contribution to effective department Attendance at and contribution to departmental meetings Contribution to department stock of teaching materials and to syllabus review
5. Administration	Department records Detentions School duties

CHECKLIST OF BASIC TASK

Describe the performance achieved for each task, include significant factors that influence results — positively or negatively. Describe strengths which contributed to the teacher's overall performance (e.g., maximizing resources, developing subordinates, decision making, interpersonal skills, and managing time). Be specific. Cite examples.

Area	Description of performance
1. Pastoral	
2. Teaching	
3. Personal skills development	
4. Departmental and school community	
5. Administration	

ADDITIONAL ACCOMPLISHMENTS

Describe also any other activities or significant accomplishments which are not reflected in the basic task or targets (e.g., contributions to the school, managing and developing staff, and administrative or curricular innovations).

TARGETS

Targets as agreed with the Head of ______________________________ Department. Targets will be mainly in the department, but could also be in house or tutor group. They could also be proposals to attend courses. They could be extra duties, e.g., clubs or societies. Targets could also include additional responsibilities or they could be for personal development, e.g., improved qualifications, experiences etc. You are advised not to exceed six topics.

The basic task: A major and assumed target is that all teaching and tutoring will be maintained at a high level. Only where there is a need for further development in one of these fields will it be listed as a target. If performance in the basic task is not satisfactory, any targets set must include a target which aims to strengthen the unsatisfactory area.

Column B = Priorities, these are: 1.Essential/2.Quite important/3.Desirable
Column C = Target date, when should the target be completed?

A Targets: What do I want to accomplish in the forthcoming academic year?	B	C	D Criteria: How will I know when I have achieved the target?	E Results achieved
Use continuation sheet if necessary				

OVERALL PERFORMANCE

Considering task performance, target achievement and any additional accomplishments, select the statement below which most accurately describes the teacher's overall performance in the past year.

Superior achievements	☐ Performance clearly surpassed expectations and substantially affected the school or department. The teacher markedly improved prior practices and/or developed new approaches.	☐ Performance clearly surpassed expectations for all targets and task requirements. The teacher improved prior practices and/or developed new approaches.
Met or exceeded high goals	☐ Got the job done by achieving all targets and task requirements and by exceeding some.	☐ Overall performance met the high standards set for teachers at this school.
Needs attention	☐ Needed on-going direction and guidance.	☐ Did not get the job done.

Areas that should be strengthened: Identify the areas that the teacher should focus on to achieve greater results. Be specific. This information will form the basis of a target for the year ahead.		
Action plan/next steps: Based on the needs above, indicate the experience and/or training planned to improve future performance. Write this up as a target now on the task-and-target sheet for next year.		
Appraiser's signature:		
Name:	Signature:	Date:
Teacher's review and signature:		
Name:	Signature:	Date:
Teacher's comments:		
Second-level review and signature:		
Name:	Signature:	Date:
Reviewer's comments:		

DOCUMENT B: TASKS-AND-TARGETS CONTINUATION SHEET

A Targets: What do I want to accomplish in the forthcoming academic year?	B	C	D Criteria: How will I know when I have achieved the target?	E Results achieved

DOCUMENT C: MEETINGS WITH DEPARTMENT HEADS

The headings on this form are intended to form the basis of our discussion. Please make your own notes on this copy, which you retain. Please make a photocopy for me of your annotated copy so that I may use it when we meet. Based on the notes and our discussion, we can together write an outline commentary on the department in general.

Headmaster

SECTION 1: THE CURRENT ACADEMIC YEAR

General	What are the current strengths of the department?
Syllabus	Has this proved satisfactory so far this year?

Organizational problems	For example: Department meetings held satisfactorily? Meetings cover all aspects of department, e.g., pupils, admin., syllabus etc.? Department work checked regularly? At what interval? Departmental record books checked regularly? At what interval? Satisfactory stock record maintained? List any problems experienced with the above or any other organizational matter.
Staffing problems	What have been the major problems with staffing this year? Are there any courses which your department ran or attended?
What has been achieved this year?	Of which aspects of the department's work do you feel most proud? Does any member of staff in the department deserve special credit this year?
Examination results	How do you expect the year's examination results to compare with last year's?

SECTION II: NEXT ACADEMIC YEAR

Syllabus	Is any revision required for the next academic year?
Staffing problems	Are there any foreseeable problems connected with staff, e.g., Are new skills needed in the department? Has preparation been made for probationers and new staff? Is the department able to take students? Please pass our decision on this to the deputy headmistress after our meeting. Are there any staff courses you would like to be able to run or attend? Are there staff in the department who would like or who need to develop certain abilities or skills? Can we discuss how this might be organized?
Finance problems	Which items in the department need to be replaced? What additions are needed? What has been missed most this year resulting from lack of capitation? What if anything did you request from the area 'pool' fund?

Room-and-space problems	How will our space problems affect the teaching in the department? What are the major needs in terms of rooms and space?
What will be the major objectives for next year in your department? Try to list them in order of priority.	

SECTION III: LONG TERM

Syllabus	Are there any proposals or developments which you would like to implement in the future?
Examinations	Are you happy with the present CSE and GCE Boards and their syllabuses? Are there any major problems ahead with implementing the new 16+ examination in your department?

Staffing problems	Are there new skills which need to be developed or added to the department? Are any courses required to help with this?
Organizational problems	Do you foresee major organizational problems in the future?
Finance problems	Are there purchases required in the long term?
Room-and-space problems	In the long term will the department suffer in any way if space or facilities are not increased? What alterations or improvements would you like to see in the long term?

DOCUMENT D: OBSERVATIONS AND CONFERENCES

Teacher's name ____________ School ________ Room ________

Subject ______________ Date ________ Period ________

S = Satisfactory/U = Unsatisfactory/NA = Not Applicable

INSTRUCTIONAL COMPETENCE

	S	U	NA
A. Planning and Preparation			
1. Realistic long-range goals exist			
2. Daily work is well planned and flexible			
3. Instruction provides for individual differences			
4. Where appropriate, pupils participate in planning			
5. Provision is made for the welfare and safety of students			
B. Learning and environment			
1. Students develop a sense of responsibility, of self-discipline, and respect for others			
2. In guiding students, the teacher uses firmness, empathy, and consistency			
3. An effective working situation and an orderly classroom are maintained			
4. The teaching station is attractive			
C. Methodology			
1. Teacher encourages students to participate in classroom discussion and activities			
2. Teacher makes certain that the students are engaged in a variety of learning experiences			
3. Teacher uses materials that are appropriate for the interests and abilities of students			
4. Teacher uses varied teaching procedures in line with specific goals of the lesson, i.e., discussions, group work, study, lectures, etc.			
5. Teacher assesses student abilities, strengths and weaknesses, and evaluates student's work as a part of the learning process			
6. Teacher assists student in appraising his or her own work			
D. Subject Matter			
1. Teacher shows concern for the student's interrelating of subject matter			
2. Teacher shows concern for practical application of subject matter			

QUALITY OF RELATIONSHIPS

A. Teacher listens to the individual student in order to understand the student's concerns and needs

B. Teacher is objective, constructive and cooperative in relations with parents

C. Teacher keeps parents informed and cooperates with them to help in the development of the student

D. Teacher cooperates with colleagues for the good of the school

1. Teacher raises questions to staff and administration in an open manner to achieve results constructively
2. Teacher collaborates in the development of curriculum objectives and goals
3. Teacher accepts and carries out staff responsibilities

PROFESSIONAL CHARACTERISTICS

A. Teacher accepts the responsibility for carrying out effective self-evaluation

B. Teacher can express differences and disagreement objectively

C. Teacher listens to ideas and criticism and weighs their merit

D. Teacher adapts successfully to changing situations

E. Teacher displays interest in new ideas, and examines them critically

F. Teacher keeps current and well informed on subject matter and methodology

G. Teacher dresses in a manner that contributes to his/her effectiveness as an educator

MANAGERIAL RESPONSIBILITIES

A. Teacher is prompt and dependable in the performance of routine matters to insure the well-being of the school

1. Reports with accuracy and depth
2. Attends promptly to office and parent communications
3. Fulfills salaried extracurricular responsibilities
4. Fulfills nonsalaried extracurricular responsibilities
5. Is punctual for appointments, assignments, and meetings
6. Requests needed instructional materials

RECOMMENDATIONS AND COMMENDATIONS

(To be completed by the evaluator)
Recommendations

Commendations

Copy to:		Signatures:
	School	
	Teacher	Evaluator ____________ Date _____
	Evaluator	
	Building principal	
	Superintendent	
	Department head	Teacher ____________ Date _____

DOCUMENT E: COUNSELLOR EVALUATION FORM

PERSONAL CHARACTERISTICS

	Self	Principal	Dept. head
1. Approaches the job or task with enthusiasm	______	______	______
2. Is self-motivated; sees what has to be done and does it	______	______	______
3. Assumes responsibility for a given task and follows through to completion	______	______	______
4. Willing to work above and beyond "normal" expectations	______	______	______
5. Dependable; does required tasks with a minimum of supervision	______	______	______
6. Persistent; doesn't give up easily on tasks	______	______	______
7. Is well-organized; has the ability to set priorities and complete work scheduled	______	______	______

8. Is punctual; shows up on time; doesn't keep others waiting ______ ______ ______

9. Is flexible; has the ability to adapt to new situations with a minimum amount of effort ______ ______ ______

10. Tolerance for ambiguity; adjusts readily to unclear situations ______ ______ ______

11. Not defensive; has the ability to look at constructive criticism objectively ______ ______ ______

12. Actively solicits feedback and incorporates it into his/her own behavior when appropriate ______ ______ ______

13. Self-awareness; conscious of his/her own feelings and behavior and how he/she affects others ______ ______ ______

14. Receptiveness; has the ability to learn from his/her own and other's experiences ______ ______ ______

15. Openness; is genuine, does not keep true feelings hidden ______ ______ ______

16. Has good judgment; decisions reflect commonsense ______ ______ ______

17. Poise and self-control; has the ability to remain calm under stress; does not "blow up" easily ______ ______ ______

18. Sense of humor; has the ability to laugh at himself/herself and to use humor in a positive way ______ ______ ______

19. Cooperative; has the ability to compromise individual effort for the common goal. Ability to work smoothly as a part of a "team-effort" ______ ______ ______

20. Has the ability to facilitate; demonstrates knowledge of group dynamics ______ ______ ______

21. Has the ability to look at problems objectively and to develop solutions ______ ______ ______

22. Has the ability to offer suggestions in a constructive and positive manner ______ ______ ______

RELATIONSHIPS WITH STUDENTS, PARENTS AND STAFF

23. Professional growth; constantly demonstrates a willingness to improve professionally ______ ______ ______

24. Promotes positive relationships between school and the community ______ ______ ______

25. Has good rapport with students ______ ______ ______

26. Demonstrates the ability to communicate with people at their "level of comfort" ______ ______ ______

27. Has good rapport with the faculty; accepted as a professional partner ______ ______ ______

28. Has good rapport with parents; accepted as a professional consultant ________ ________ ________

29. Has a good working relationship with administrators ________ ________ ________

GUIDANCE PROGRAM

30. Constantly works towards development of a balanced guidance program:

a. Provides individual counseling opportunities ________ ________ ________

b. Provides group counseling opportunities ________ ________ ________

c. Provides guidance activities for all students (testing, information, placement services, etc.) ________ ________ ________

d. Provides adequate orientation services ________ ________ ________

e. Handles referrals efficiently and effectively ________ ________ ________

f. Understands his/her own professional limitations (knows when to refer a client to someone else) ________ ________ ________

g. Maintains accurate and up-to-date records ________ ________ ________

h. Well aware of available resources in and out of the district ________ ________ ________

i. Conducts follow-up and research activities on a regular basis ________ ________ ________

31. Works closely with administrative staff in the development of a positive learning environment in the schools: ________ ________ ________

a. Provides regular in-put for curriculum revision ________ ________ ________

b. Constantly reminds staff and administration of individual needs of all students ________ ________ ________

c. Assists teachers in development of individualized programs for students with special needs ________ ________ ________

d. Develops in-service programs to meet the needs of staff ________ ________ ________

7 INTRODUCING AND SERVICING THE SYSTEM

> There is nothing more difficult to take in hand, more perilous to conduct or more uncertain in its success than to take the lead in the introduction of a new order of things.
>
> Machiavelli, *The Prince*

The successful introduction of appraisals demands preparation in two main directions: winning commitment; and designing appraisal training.

WINNING COMMITMENT

Even if teacher appraisal is introduced into English and Welsh schools through 'enabling powers' granted by Parliament to the Secretary of State for Education and Science, it could rapidly decline into an operational façade unless there is a clear commitment to it by those staff who manage others. This commitment must be obvious in those introducing the system, and time must be spent 'selling' the system and persuading both the appraiser and appraised that its advantages accrue more certainly when it is operated with commitment.

Let us now assume that an LEA has decided upon the form of appraisal it wishes to introduce and its target date. It has agreed the purpose of 'improved teacher performance' as its central aim and clarified its accountabilities, and its routines and draft-appraisal documentation has been prepared. Let us further assume that the LEA project team which devised the scheme took account of the views of all hierarchical levels within its schools, all sizes and nature of schools and of the views of unions and professional associations. It also took the advice of an external consultant, not from industry but from a school with direct successful personal experience of teacher appraisal. The LEA appraisal-project team now recommends that in each school a team of staff be appointed under the chairmanship of headteacher to introduce the system into that school. An external consultant would be available for advice to each school, either from the LEA's own existing advisory service or from a number of especially appointed appraisal assessors, as recommended in the Suffolk report.

The first stage for each school is to select the people who will be responsible for introducing the system. They will form the team of initiators and their commitment to the appraisal system being introduced is essential. This group will make the change happen. It should number between three and ten team members, and staff should be selected as initiators more for their personal qualities than as representatives of hierarchical levels within the school or as union or group representatives. Ideally such initiators should be good, general 'presenters' of information, and it is essential that they are comfortable when discussing appraisals on a one-to-one or small-group basis. Anyone who feels uncomfortable with this situation of possible close personal questioning or who does not generate trust and understanding when meeting people eyeball to eyeball will not be a good advocate for appraisals. They should also be easily able to see things from the point of view of others.

The initiators should aim to be accepted by the staff not only for their willingness to listen to teachers' reservations about the scheme but for their depth of understanding of it. Staff should be saying of the initiators, 'These are people we can really talk to. They listen and talk us through our reservations, they really know the job we do at school and they thoroughly understand the purposes and practices of the appraisal system.' How will teacher contact be made?

1. Whole staff meetings: sometimes it is advantageous to divide into discussion syndicates to allow greater depth of discussion, bringing reports, or flipchart summaries or 'key questions for discussion' back to the full staff session to gain an impression of the full staff view.

2. Team meetings: These will be near the heart of the new appraisal system. It is essential that team members bring into the open any reservation they have about being appraised in the particular team in which they work.

3. One-to-one meetings: Appraisal itself will depend heavily on the success of one-to-one meetings. Therefore initiators need to show the same kind of skills, patience and understanding at this introductory stage as will be needed to run the scheme later on. It is no good trying to force the pace at this stage; if this is attempted, doors are closed. It is only possible to go at the speed which others are willing to take when an answer or a reassurance cannot be quickly provided for a teacher. The most important skill for the initiator to show is the understanding of the teacher's problems.

The purpose of this first phase of the introduction of an LEA scheme into school is twofold: to give teachers knowledge about the appraisal scheme; and to bring into the open the underlying fears, hostilities and suspicions about the scheme.

Initiators should be ready for fears expressed both overtly and covertly. People will be asking themselves: What's behind this? How am I going to be affected by these changes? What shall I have to do to come to terms with this situation? Will I be able to measure up to it? However, their statements to the initiators may be much more indirect. Well-established objections to hide such real fears are: 'We tried a scheme like this before'; or, 'It wouldn't work here.' Yet another cover for real fears is the technical objection to some part of the scheme: 'Ah, but I'm only used to teaching Geography. I don't know how to turn my work into tasks and targets.' Such comments may need to be discussed on two levels: the superficial technical level and the more subtle underlying one of personal anxiety about the scheme.

It is not true that provided you give enough information and let people know what is going on, things will work out right. The importance of this initial phase is the opportunity it must provide for teachers to express their underlying fears. As these fears appear there will be general fears about change, being superceded, being devalued, being worse off. The general answer in these cases is to show people how they can contribute to the change and how their skills and experience will still be valued, maybe even more so.

A typical exercise carried out at this stage with several groups of teachers, headteachers and LEA officials and advisers is to set syndicate groups discussing these points:

1. State the principal objectives of a staff appraisal system
2. Identify the likely barriers to achieving these objectives
3. Provide your recommendations for the removal of these barriers

When other more direct approaches have not encouraged expression of fears, a set of points phrased in a more general way such as these may draw forth more personal reservations couched in terms of the third person plural. Replies to point 2, for example, have been listed on flipcharts as: 'The staff may be worried about confidentiality'; 'Teachers may be worried about the credibility of the appraisers'; or 'People may wonder what is going to be done with the information.'

Such concerns then need to be explored by the initiator to show that the scheme designers have considered these issues and provided solutions. Not every underlying fear will be expressed, but unless initiators genuinely try to understand and work through to a satisfactory conclusion those real and apparent fears which can be identified will remain as stumbling blocks when the scheme is implemented.

This, we know, is the stage at which we give knowledge but not skills training to those in the scheme. One group in particular is crucial to the success of the scheme — the group who not only will be appraised but will appraise its own team and set targets with them. In medium to large schools these team leaders will be departmental heads. It is they who must be able to appraise their departmental colleagues; only they truly know whether criteria set for targets with their teachers are realistic. At this stage they do not yet have to possess the skill to do this, but they must be sufficiently committed to make or help to make appraisal happen. Since 100% commitment of all teachers in all schools is too high a target to set, the critical group is the group of departmental heads. Commitment from their departmental colleagues is an extra; we can begin with some, possibly many, of the staff being merely willing to endure the change. Mere compliance will suffice at the start. If the system is as good as it claims to be, going along with it will in itself win commitment.

Team leaders therefore need more time spent on gaining knowledge of the system's operation. They need to test their understanding of the system more thoroughly, for example:

1. By completing the mock-ups of the appraisal forms. Do they see operating problems? Do they see the problems created by not completing them properly?
2. By identifying operating problems. Although the strategic decisions have been taken, can team leaders make suggestions about the operation of the system at a tactical level?
3. By preparing answers to likely questions, for example, a quick-quiz on the key features of the appraisal system — especially of those points his or her departmental team may want to check on

So, our aim at the end of this first introductory stage is a high percentage of commitment to the scheme especially from its operators. Clearly, the headteacher and the remainder of the initiator group must be committed, but so too must be all those who will appraise others, in particular, leaders of departmental teams. Most, if not all, underlying fears have been resolved; there is a high level of knowledge of how the appraisal scheme will operate and team leaders have added their tactical refinements to the plan. We now need skills training.

DESIGNING APPRAISAL TRAINING

The first stage in designing appraisal training is to build an audit of the needs of the teachers if they are to be able to meet the job requirements. In respect of appraisal, teachers must first be made aware of what is required and involved and must next be asked to identify skills which they feel they lack and the tasks likely to prove most difficult for them and why. Staff entirely unaware of appraisal skills may need to begin with elementary awareness training which shows by demonstration, example and discussion what is intended to happen in the appraisal process. Many teachers, however, will be aware and may even have begun to feel the need of particular skills training. Not all needs can be met by appraisal training. If teachers feel that one great need is additional time to perform appraisals then this information is for consideration by the LEA. Nevertheless, such a request may conceal the fact that teachers are spending far too long on appraisals and for that reason need training or a refresher course in the basic appraisal-interview skills.

The simplest form of a 'needs' survey is a questionnaire which asks those teachers who will conduct appraisal what they believe to be their greatest training need. It will probably be helpful to them to suggest headings under which needs can be identified, for example: skills; knowledge; time; support; experiences; any other aspect.

A second stage in designing appraisal training is to compile the surveys into an audit of training needs. To this consumer-based audit can be added information gained from observation elsewhere of appraisals in operation in schools. Analyze the total audit and from it deduce specific behaviour objectives and purposes for training.

The next stage is to design training situations to achieve these objectives, and a complete two-day training course for teacher appraisers is included as Appendix III. The chief design considerations for appraisal training concern situations, organization and materials.

Situations

- Create the situation where people can behave effectively and where this can be acknowledged.
- Introduce conflict and action; skills training implies activity.
- Use simulated *not* real situations which are known to the participants from their own schools.

Organization

The major considerations are:

- Multiple simultaneous action by all group members or single group with spectators?
- Structured or unstructured simulation?
- Role multiplicity (e.g., coaches, stand-ins, etc.) or only appraiser, appraisee and observer?

- Amount of verbal or nonverbal emphasis: Is nonverbal communication being considered as a facet of appraisal?

Materials

- Keep the background and instructions simple and brief.
- Give hints on how a role should be played to achieve the aim of the session.
- Give a written brief or verbal instruction to observers so that they will look for the appropriate skills.

If the needs have been identified as 'dealing effectively with teachers who are not performing satisfactorily' and 'negotiating targets with under-achieving teachers', then probably structured simulations will meet the training need. These may need case studies designed, training videos created and observers' sheets specially written. These materials should be tested to see how far they are likely to achieve their purpose, and if necessary the material improved. Materials can be tested on other trainers or on a control group of teachers. Finally, not only should the materials give appropriate training, but they should be included in a programme which induces appropriate discussion of the problem.

TRAINING FOR APPRAISAL

Ask any group of teachers to consider their fears about teacher appraisal, and high on the list of both appraiser and appraised will appear reservations such as: 'lack of appraisal skills'; 'rules of the appraisal room need negotiating'; 'how will the credibility of appraisers be established?' 'lack of teacher confidence in the appraiser'.

These hurried jottings taken from teachers at actual appraisal training sessions, highlight the need for appraisers to develop their appraisal interview techniques and for all teachers to be at least comfortably aware of how appraisal interviews are conducted.

The format of actual interviews, the styles used in interview and the techniques for achieving the purpose of the interview have already been discussed. What is now needed is an outline of the most suitable forms of training which can be used to develop the interviewers' skills. In ten years of interpersonal skills training I have found no more effective technique than simulation, and in particular, role-play simulation.

PREPARING FOR SIMULATION

Interpersonal simulation can best be handled with between 5 and 15 people led by a trainer. With larger numbers training is less effective because fewer teachers can be directly involved and tend to become mere spectators. Spectating, being a relatively passive role, is not as effective as participating, which is active, in interpersonal skills training.

It is essential to establish an ethos for the training which is spontaneous, open, freely experimenting and freely exchanging of information. There must be no feeling that the participants are being evaluated or punished in any way.

WHAT FORMS CAN SIMULATION TRAINING TAKE?

Simulation is an attempt to create certain environmental or other real-life conditions for training purposes. Within the simulated conditions teachers can be given the opportunity to solve problems, practice skills or, in general, to behave as they would or should if faced with these conditions at school.

The dummy run

The dummy-run technique asks the appraiser to demonstrate the difficulty he or she is experiencing or expects to experience in conducting an appraisal interview. This is frequently used in appraisal training to check on unhelpful practices or styles being used by an appraiser. Having identified the practice, a new technique can be developed and again tested at a dummy-run session. There, the trainer requires maximum control so that extraneous factors do not detract from the 'test' situation. This is a good method for improving the techniques of experienced appraisers.

Pilot projects

Pilot projects are most frequently used in appraisal training by trainers to test out a new approach or technique before offering it more widely to trainee appraisers.

Models and games

The forms of simulation which provide a contextual framework into which other subject matter can be fed are models and games. Known variables in an actual situation are identified and a hypothetical model is set up in which these variables are expected to operate.

Probably the least effective in appraisal training are computerized models which, although they can simulate time pressures and the stresses and strains of team work, are mainly cognitive in their simulations rather than emotional. Computer simulations can be used to set up a situation and give an impartial decision on any action taken, but cannot simulate the emotional environment. For example, a question in a computerized objective test on appraisal interviewing may ask:

In an interview which you are conducting a teacher becomes angry at your appraisal of his or her performance as a tutor. Do you

(a) quickly change your view of the performance to align with the teacher's view?
(b) ask the teacher to present his or her views in the form of a self-appraisal?
(c) tell the teacher to like it or lump it?

A trainee appraiser may well select option (b), but it has given that trainee no indication of how he or she would react personally and emotionally when conducting an appraisal which is going badly wrong.

Much more widely used in general school-management training is the literary model — a fictional written account of the school history and biography of its staff over a period of years. Setting appraisal training in this context sometimes makes it easier for trainees to role play.

Structured interpersonal techniques

In structured simulations, the trainers have determined beforehand the objectives of the training and the critical relationships with which the participants are expected to cope.

The most inflexible of these techniques is the prerecorded appraisal interview. This can be examined to search for breakdown points, examples of bad technique and of poor listening or for the more positive reverse of these features. There is a little more involvement in using a transcribed script of the recorded interview. Two course participants can come closer to the feeling created by conducting the interview by reading the scripted roles, but in a situation in which the words used are not their own. At some point, having partly read the script, it is highly likely that both will be willing to lay aside the script and continue the appraisal using their own personal interpretation of the role. The participants have moved into one of the most familiar and valuable forms of appraisal simulations — group assignment role-plays.

In group assignment role-plays the roles, background and procedures are planned prior to the session. The most common form is one in which all members practise the appraisal skills in turn whilst others assess the appraiser's performance. The appraisee role can be played by the trainer or rotated among group members. If a spontaneous, open and freely experimenting atmosphere has been created this form of simulation is an outstandingly good method of correcting predetermined appraisal-interview technique problems.

One further simulation form depends even more upon the trainer's ability to create an appropriate atmosphere. This is the unstructured simulation situation in which the problems, the situations and techniques are not predetermined, but emerge from the group. For example, a trainer may say, 'The aim today is to deal with the situation of a difficult complaint arising during an appraisal interview. Can anyone give an example?' On being given the example the trainer continues 'Will you select someone to play the complainant and briefly show us the approach you take.' By questioning in this way the trainer establishes the day, place, time, and the simulated activity begins. It is this situation with which the trainer deals during the training session.

Variations within the unstructured simulation mode allow for trainees to swop roles or for each role player to have a coach, with whom he or she can discuss progress and tactics during the interview. Another variation is to allow interruption to the simulated action whenever a useful suggestion can be made.

Clearly the choice of the simulation form lies with the trainer and will be partly influenced by his or her own confidence and experience. However, many advantages in using interpersonal simulation are:

1. Can be enjoyable.
2. Can be highly credible if overplaying is avoided.
3. Can be flexible in technique since it can be easily changed, edited or ended.
4. Can be flexible in time and place. With very few props a course can be set up and run almost anywhere.
5. Puts the emphasis on skills-based learning within a context, so reducing resistance to learning relevant skills in the abstract.
6. Decisions can be tested without the consequences of taking them in real situations.
7. Uses the experiences of the participants to a large extent.
8. Raises the participants awareness of the need for interpersonal skills.
9. Runs at a relatively low cost.

However, there are some disadvantages in using interpersonal simulation for appraisal interview training. Chief among these may be:

1. The 'nonreal-life' nature of the work may discourage appreciation of its value.

2. Can be threatening for some people.
3. Can encourage stereotyping and caricature.
4. Can deteriorate into 'play' if not skilfully handled.
5. Spectators may learn little unless observing or coaching.

PREPARING FOR A STRUCTURED SIMULATION

The basic format for any simulation consists of: climate setting; action; feedback; generalizing; and applying. In structured simulations the trainer identifies the purposes prior to the session and determines behavioural objectives as part of the design of the course.

Climate setting

Climate setting consists of orienting the trainees towards the topic. A possible opening is one which sets the course in its current context. For example, 'As you know, the new pay structure which has been negotiated will soon require teachers to be skilled in performance appraisal. We hope today to identify the skills involved in this practice and to raise them in each one of us to a level of operational competence.' This could be supported with any or all of the following:

(a) A brief lecture on the advantages to individual and school of regular performance appraisal

(b) A video illustrating appraisal skills or styles (e.g., Video Arts *How Am I Doing*?)

(c) A case study, showing how performance could have been improved by use of regular appraisal

This opening should be followed by a discussion to focus attention on problems which will be tackled in the simulation. Discussion questions might include: How do you feel about the possible introduction of appraisals? What do you fear could go wrong in an appraisal situation? What conditions would make it easy for you to feel positively about appraisal?

The trainer might then list the key issues which the group feels are important in an appraisal interview. For example,

- Preparation by the appraiser
- Sufficient notice to the appraisee
- Appraiser to be a skilled listener
- Appraiser to be a fair negotiator
- An accurate summary needed
- An accurate report kept

Action — Steps in the simulation

STEP 1: Provide background and assign the roles

The most effective form of background is a case study. Two examples of cases suitable for use with the introduction of appraisals into a school are given at the end of this chapter. The trainer must decide whether to:

(a) Have multiple or single-group action (e.g., 1 × 15, 3 × 5, 5 × 3)
(b) Use separate rooms or to operate within one large room
(c) Issue background sheets to outline the case
(d) Issue role briefings

STEP 2: Provide for interventions

The next stage of planning is for the trainer to decide from either (a), (b) or (c) how interventions will be made:

(a) Observers to intervene: The key skills are presented to all trainees by lecture, film or by demonstration. Observers are given behaviour-rating sheets and provide feedback on the simulation against the rating sheet which highlight the predetermined skills, issues and objectives.

(b) Role rotation or reversal: Observers may illustrate a point by assuming a role in the simulation or by asking the role players to reverse roles. Feedback from the participants may trigger role rotation or reversal, even when not planned. For example, 'I thought you role-played the appraiser well except when you had to get the teacher to face facts about her promotion chances. I would have preferred a more direct approach. Shall I show you what I mean?'

(c) Other solutions: At the end of one simulation other solutions which have been reached in earlier simulations on the same topic can be offered by the leader and discussed by the group. Another possibility is that the group can be asked to propose and discuss other solutions.

STEP 3: Do it again

(a) The same simulation can be used again after feedback and discussion. This gives the participants feedback on techniques which they can use in their improved form of replay. Skills can be improved in this active form of simulation even without direct feedback or analysis, but in general feedback should be structured to be present.

(b) Points for discussion after the repeated simulation

- Does the participant feel that performance actually improved?
- Does the participant feel more satisfied, confident, and so forth?
- Do observers receive the impression that the simulation successfully improved performance?
- Does a video recording convey improved performance?

In structured situations the feedback occasion from an observer based upon behaviour-rating sheets is built into the session.

Feedback

The observers next make their comments, aided by the trainer. This feedback from an observer and based upon observations recorded on the behaviour-rating sheets is built into the session. It is extremely important to ensure the process does not become highly critical or evaluative.

Trainers should encourage trainee appraisers to: experiment with new behaviours; become aware of the feelings of the participants; and encourage spontaneity.

Generalizing

The trainer should ask for positive feedback, for example, What did the appraiser do that you thought was very effective? or how did the appraiser show that he was listening? Also, the trainer should focus on the procedure *not* the person, for example, Which of our key techniques did you see demonstrated in that interview? and which technique might have been stressed in that session?

Applying

In the final session the trainer should ask the trainees two questions: first, So what? (i.e., What has this simulation to do with real life?); and, second, Now what? (i.e., What do I do to use these skills in real life?).

The aim is to bring the trainee back from the training session to real life at school. The link between training and actual will be an action plan. Every trainee should be encouraged to produce a draft action plan before leaving the training module.

USES OF SIMULATION IN GENERAL APPRAISAL TRAINING

Learning a method

Familiarize trainees with specific methods, whether of handling interviews, completing forms, observing lessons etc.

Handling human relations problems

Familiarize trainees with methods of handling human-relations problems which occur both in the appraisal interview and in the general management of colleagues.

In self-awareness training

Make the trainee appraiser aware of his or her own strengths and weaknesses as an appraiser and manager of others.

In demonstrating or clarifying a principle or technique

Either the trainer or the trainee can demonstrate a principle or technique, thus making more explicit than by any other method their intention.

In analysis

Following a simulated appraisal it is possible to analyze how a trainee performs in certain situations and by simulating situations which are yet to arise can also analyze how the trainee is likely to perform ahead of reality and so permit precautionary training.

EFFECTIVE LISTENING

One fundamental skill of appraisal interviewing is the appraiser's ability to listen effectively, especially when confronted with disagreement or resistance. Its training is easy to arrange. An exercise in listening training is given as Document B at the end of this chapter.

OTHER TRAINING TECHNIQUES

Although simulation is strongly advocated as an outstanding vehicle for meeting the needs of those wishing to acquire appraisal skills, it is not the only approach or technique available. Of certain value, especially in the acquisition of knowledge as opposed to the acquisition of skills, are the more didactic approaches of reading and listening to lectures. Other techniques in the order in which they become increasingly experiential are: discussion groups; experiential lectures; case studies, whether acted out or discussed; surveys; structured experiences; counselling and therapy.

Role playing would join the preceding at about the level of case studies. The choice of which training mode to use has to be left to the skill and experience of the trainer, bearing mind, as he or she will, the maturity and experience of the trainees, their learning needs, the time available and the environment in which the training takes place.

Finally, no self-respecting trainer would allow a course to end without obtaining the feedback of the participants. This information is most valuable in considering the course successes and weaknesses and any improvements which may need to be made. Since the trainer is trying to convey the skills of appraisal, there is all the more reason to seek an assessment of the training from course members.

There are two key occasions for obtaining feedback on whole courses and even of individual sessions. The first is immediately upon its conclusion; though there is a risk of euphoria, at that time following a successful course, a quick reaction-questionnaire completed by all members will give the immediate impression left in the minds of members. An example is Document C at the end of this chapter.

The second occasion for obtaining feedback is about six months after the completion of the course. Then, a more reflective report can be taken up, broadly asking the participants to indicate the items in the course which have been of lasting value and those which have disappointed in the longer term. Both forms of feedback will help the trainer to go on improving and developing his or her appraisal courses.

SAMPLE DOCUMENTS

DOCUMENT A: TWO CASE STUDIES

If the context of a particular school is required by the discussing group, would the leader either discuss the situation as if it were in the school of one of the group members, or make the necessary assumptions about context as situations arise.

CASE STUDY NO. 1: TOM BRAGSBY

Tom Bragsby is a Scale 1 BEd mathematician, newly married, aged 24, with one year's teaching experience. He passed his probationary year very successfully. He found teaching suited him admirably. His discipline is sound, his relationships with pupils are good, though staff find him a little conceited and irritating. All his work in the Mathematics Department is prepared and marked well. He teaches effectively, and it is clear from all his internal and external examination results, that he has the ability to teach well. His administration is first class in all aspects of school life. He has one weakness with pupils, which is a tendency to become too informal, and then to overreact if pupils are informal in return. During one incident he overreacted and struck a boy on the nose. He bitterly regretted the incident, though still tends to flare up from time to time. A further weakness is pointed out by his head of house who fears that his tutor group, unlike his mathematics class, is often in disorder and while he is perfectly willing to involve himself with small groups of pupils, the remainder of the tutor group gives the impression of chaos. He hopes to gain promotion in the academic field, and attaches minimal importance to pastoral tutoring.

Tom is keen to accept responsibility for training, running and arranging fixtures for a school rugby team and take them to matches on a tour of South Wales. He has also offered to lead a school trip to California where he has recently been undertaking summer holiday work in a youth holiday camp. He is now approaching the midpoint of his second year teaching. What objectives would you wish to set with him for the next twelve months if you were Tom's head of department? As headteacher or deputy what advice would you offer?

CASE STUDY NO. 2: JOHN SCRAWN

John Scrawn is a graduate history teacher, aged 53, with 17 years' teaching experience, all in his present school. He is married, with four children all over 20. He was a late entry at 36 into the profession from the Church. He is a knowledgeable teacher but ever since his none too successful probationary year, his head of department and head of house have carefully selected only the most malleable of pupils for his groups. He seems unaware of the poor reputation for discipline he has acquired. This is very evident in his dealing with a broader range of children, for example, on duty or at lunch-time or when acting as a substitute.

He is now pressing for promotion, and is uncharacteristically moody with senior colleagues at his lack of success. He is considering joining a course for aspiring heads of departments, and has undertaken two counselling courses and a pastoral-care course.

John is a caring tutor, much liked by his tutorial group, though they can pull the wool over his eyes when they wish. He has no tutor-programme organization, but it would be unfair to say that he did not know his tutor group well or that his personal relationship with them was not good and pleasant.

John's administrative qualities are fair, though he tends to be lax over some matters, such as keeping a pupil after school without notice of detention, failing to complete assessments on time and being late at meetings.

He contributes well to the life of the school but never in a leading role. He is always willing to help anyone in distress, to be versatile for the sake of timetable construction and to join in any social activity be it choir, school visit, theatre visit or party. Teetotal, nonsmoking, and heavily overweight even for his six-foot frame, he feels he has been by-passed in life. His departmental head has found it easier to 'work round' John, sorting out only those problems which demand attention.

As head or deputy of the school, please suggest some course of action to deal with this problem.

DOCUMENT B: EFFECTIVE LISTENING EXERCISE

Divide the group into threes. One member is designated an appraiser (member A), another is to be an appraisee (member B) and the third is to be an observer (member C).

BRIEFING FOR MEMBER B (APPRAISEE)

During the exercise you are to express your opinions freely. If you encounter resistance or disagreement you may deal with it any way you see fit. You are asked not to role play but to express your genuine feelings about the issue and pursue your point of view to clarify the issue, influence the other person's opinion, or simply get your own position stated. You are to initiate the discussion by introducing your point of view about this statement. Then list a series of statements, one of which the member is likely to have fairly strong views about, for example,

- Primary teachers, pupils and schools are unfairly treated by most LEAs compared with the equivalent secondary group.
- Money is the only universal motivator of teaching profession.
- Men dominate in all organizations. They are chauvinistic and unfair towards women.

BRIEFING FOR MEMBER A (APPRAISER)

Your task in this activity is to listen and ask questions and understand. Do not press your own opinion or defend it or try to convert the other person to your viewpoint. You may, from time to time, state ideas. The following suggestions are provided to guide you in this listening exercise:

1. Ask general questions (What do you think? What happened?) to find out more about what another person thinks. Beware of leading or loaded questions or questions that lead to a predetermined answer.
2. Use statements that encourage the person to talk. (Tell me more about it; I'm interested in some of your other feelings.) These tend to increase disclosure.
3. Try paraphrasing responses that pick up from what the other person has said and feed it back as a question. For example, if a person says 'I think men are too abrasive and oppressive in trying to win promotion', you might say, 'I see. You think that men are very aggressive in the way in which they pursue their targets?' This kind of response encourages the other person to talk and shows you are listening.

BRIEFING FOR MEMBER 'C' (OBSERVER)

During the course of the discussion, observe member A. Did he or she

- Quickly reveal his or her own point of view and push for a favourite point?
- Ask questions that suggest a desired answer (leading or loaded questions)?
- Seem interested in drawing out and understanding the viewpoint of the other?
- Occasionally paraphrase what the other person said or use other nondirective techniques to draw out additional information?
- Defend his or her own viewpoint?

Comment on ways in which the interviewer kept the discussion going.

DOCUMENT C: SESSION ASSESSMENT

Title of Course: ____________________ Name: ________________________

Title of Session: ____________________

Date: ____________________

For each of the questions 1–5, will you please place a tick (: :) above the point on the scale corresponding to your opinion about the session you have attended

1. How much did you enjoy the session as a whole?
   very stimulating :____:____:____:____:____:____:____: very boring
2. To what extent have you been able to understand the material presented?
   completely :____:____:____:____:____:____:____: I found it all rather confusing
3. How important do you think it is for you to remember what you have learnt in this session?
   extremely important :____:____:____:____:____:____:____: totally unnecessary

4. To what extent will you be able to apply what you have learnt in this session to your job?

able to apply most :____:____:____:____:____:____:____: unable to apply any

5. How would you comment on the overall presentation of the session?

excellent :____:____:____:____:____:____:____: poor

Please write any other comments below (and overleaf if required) e.g., whether the session lived up to your expectations; how could it be improved etc.

8 APPRAISING THE HEAD

> It sure as hell would lack credibility if the Principals and Superintendents weren't appraised.
>
> Suffolk Education Department, 1985

Who should appraise headteachers? One cardinal rule of this book is that 'feedback without responsibility' is *not* appraisal. Feedback is useful but unless it is feedback from someone who has the task of managing and appraising the teacher's performance, then it can be ignored, and probably will be by the least effective performers. Exactly the same principle applies to headteachers. The only complicating factor is that headteachers receive feedback from such a variety of sources and are not given feedback by sources to which they appear to be accountable so that an illusion of accountability and appraisal of headteachers is created — 'Appraisal by trompe l'oeil', a *Times Educational Supplement* cartoon called it.

This is not to underrate the value of feedback to a headteacher from any source. The alert head, intent on developing the school will take feedback from any quarter. Some he or she will accept, some will be rejected as untrue, some will be picked over and accepted selectively, ruling out feedback which seems tainted by prejudice and bias. Much, however, whether positive or negative will be welcomed by the alert headteacher and will be acted upon. But the plain truth is that any head who is sufficiently insensitive, determined or obdurate, need not act upon any of this feedback at all. Ask any interested but practically powerless group affected by a headteacher's performance whether their feedback to him or her brings about a change. Ask parents or teachers or governors how effective their feedback to a poorly performing headteacher of an underachieving school has been, and it will be seen how ineffective is this 'appraisal without responsibility'.

Let us look briefly at who gives the head and the school this form of feedback. Lyn Jones, the Chief Educational Officer of Hillingdon produced an analysis of what he calls the 'client groups' for schools. Lyn Jones says that Hillingdon schools

> largely of their own volition, as a matter of social, moral and pedagogic responsibility, are very fully mindful of the needs, demands and expectations of all the 'client groups' to which they are in one way or another properly answerable.

His diagram of 'pressures and interactions' shows the client groups to be the DES, the education committee, the local council, H.M. Inspectorate, employees, advisers, members of Parliament, local councillors, outside statutory agencies, local professional associations, local pressure groups, individual citizens, parents, LEA officers and governors. Schools throughout Britain serve these same client groups and may choose to be responsive to some degree to the pressures from them on their school.

Effective schools keep up a dialogue with all such clients largely because they give feedback on headteacher and school performance as they see it. But is there any way in which their possible conflicting demands upon schools can become agreed school policy except through the 'balancing' of these pressures by the head? Does any person or committee claim to manage the headteacher and to give a meaningful appraisal of his or her performance? My attempt as a headteacher to identify my own manager is reported elsewhere (Trethowan, 1981). A dozen separate sets of feedback from client groups creates unnecessary conflict for the sensitive head who tries to respond to them all and allows the Machiavellian head to play one group off against another while proceeding along a self-determined course.

Who should manage and appraise the head? Governors are the most obvious group to be expected to manage and appraise the head, but all too few of these busy lay people have either the time or the expertise to do so. Seldom do they have both. Nor are governors fully accountable for the performance of a head. Most governing bodies change in composition long before they are able to reap what they might encourage a headteacher to sow. None of these obstacles prevents governors, either as a body or individually, giving valuable feedback to the headteacher. Many heads believe that some of their most valuable discussions on school objectives and management are with the experienced, able, informed men and women who serve as governors. But governors do not hold a line management relationship with the head and cannot therefore give 'appraisal with responsibility' if they are not charged with responsibility for the headteacher. There is seldom a claim from such a body to be the manager of a headteacher, guiding and appraising his or her performance, setting and reviewing the head's targets and accepting fully accountable responsibility for that headteacher's performance.

For a proposal which brings governing bodies closer to the role of managing and appraising the headteacher see 'Industrial Means to Educational Ends' (Trethowan, 1985b).

How close to that managerial role is the Parents Association? Many of the same strengths apply to this body as to governors. But so do the same weaknesses, with the further danger of bias in the parent towards decisions which may improve the prospects of their own children at the expense of others. Even if these objections could be laid aside, should a body such as this accept responsibility for managing the performance of a headteacher? Could it not be argued that schools belong to society at large, not to any group within society? Decisions on the structure of schools and on their curricula are community decisions. Since the community's voice is expressed in a democracy through bodies elected by the community then it is these national and local bodies which have this decision-making duty.

A further duty of elected representatives is the management of the performance of the Chief Education Officer as chief executive of the education service to ensure that community policy is carried out in the most effective manner. It is my personal belief that this chief executive should appoint an agent to manage the performance of headteachers and to conduct their appraisal and target-setting sessions. This is exactly the role of school superintendent in the USA, where accountability to the community is held dear. I have continually advocated the adoption of this role by the British education system since undertaking a tour of US schools in 1978, and published such a recommendation some time afterwards (Trethowan, 1981). The Suffolk research-study report confirms this view by providing recommendations for headteacher appraisal which exactly match the duties of school superintendent.

> We would recommend:
> (a) headteachers must be appraised
> (b) a clearly defined, realistic line of management must be established
> (c) in order to know the work of the head, the appraiser should be experienced in the task of headship
> (d) a level of 'promoted' head should be established for this work [Suffolk Education Department, 1985]

In the USA superintendents are themselves both experienced administrators and former heads of schools with recent exposure to the rigours and wrinkles of school management. The need for a school superintendent who knows the job is endorsed by others.

> But it is critical that a manager know enough about the job and the work environment so that he or she can articulate reasonable performance objectives to the performer, provide the necessary resources, arrange appropriate consequences and supply relevant performance feedback. If he or she can't do that, all the human-relations training in the world won't make him or her a successful manager [Morgan, Hall and Mackay, 1983]

Indeed, this experience of headship strengthens their administration and assists in a realistic interpretation of policy. No administrator successfully administers what he or she does not truly understand.

The layman might well ask if the role being proposed for this school superintendent is not already being filled by local inspectors and advisers, by H.M. Inspectorate and by the Education Administration Service. Far from it. Local inspectors and advisers may give the layman the impression of being the roving managers of schools, but they themselves never claim the role. They have a different brief, they are too few, have too little time, and in general have a marked lack of headship or of managerial experience. It may be unfair to repeat the joke amongst headteachers that advisers only drop in at schools for advice, but there is an element of truth in this. Their strengths lie in these directions: liaison, pragmatism, explaining policy, and cross-fertilizing valuable feedback between schools but certainly not in assuming responsibility for the performance of headteachers.

Does the national H.M. Inspectorate fulfil this appraising and managerial role for heads? Not at all. H.M. inspectors bring incisive, publicized but fleeting visits from ephemeral experts on school and staff performance. Valuable as their reports are, coming as they do from a service which has a high reputation amongst the teaching profession, they are far from any form of management or appraisal of headteacher performance. Firstly, 'feedback with responsibility' is lacking, and secondly, a visit from the H.M. Inspectorate occurs too rarely in the headteachers' professional lifetime for them to be managed by any member of this service.

None of the more recently proposed solutions to the problem of headteacher appraisal meets the requirements of 'feedback with responsibility'. Official suggestions for appraising headteachers vary from peer appraisal to team appraisal. Peer appraisal is the appraisal of a headteacher by other local headteachers. Even if this feedback on performance were well intentioned, accurate and true, how much time can one head devote to giving regular and frequent feedback on the performance of another? Some heads still see other local heads as rivals, others as chums; either view might distort the appraisal of a performance for which the appraiser was not accountable. As feedback, if it worked, it could be valuable. As a form of effective appraisal it is a dead duck.

Team appraisal is a form of mutual appraisal by the headteacher, the deputy heads and the local advisers. This has much to commend it. By drawing in the deputies the feedback on headteacher performance could be well informed, accurate and incisive. But by making it mutual appraisal the team members are being encouraged to scratch each other's back for the benefit of an onlooking adviser. Who in the team is responsible for the performance of the other? Surely they all have a duty to give each other feedback, but appraisal requires much more than this.

In April 1986, the Committee of Heads of Education Institutions (CHEI) made its proposal for the appraisal of heads. After agreeing that headteacher appraisal has its benefits, CHEI proposed the creation of an initial cadre of professional appraisers, carefully matched to the type of headship to be appraised. The system is summarized as:

> 1. Four people would be directly involved:
> (a) The independent Professional Appraiser, who should be directly responsible for the appraisal, should write it and sign it together with the Head, who would have the right of access to the Senior Chief Inspector on matters requiring a second level appraiser.
> (b) The Professional Appraiser would be briefed in the appraisal by:
> (i) The Chief Education Officer [CEO], or his senior representative;
> (ii) The Chairman of Governors;
> (iii) Member of the teaching staff of the institution elected for this purpose.
> 2. Appraisal should take place at least every three years.
> 3. The process of appraisal should take place over a period of up to three days.
> 4. The three days might include:
> Day 1: Discussion with the CEO, Chairman of Governors, staff representative. Tour of premises, discussion with staff and students.
> Day 2: Professional Appraiser with Head.
> Day 3: Compiling report.
> 5. Since the object of the triennial exercise is to encourage, above all, the development of the individual, we do not see it as calling for something in the nature of the report delivered to a governing body by an HMI after a general inspection. Monitoring of standards and performance through inspections, reports to governors, and in other ways are quite separate matters and would continue by existing means. The appraiser's report on the Head will be confidential and personal and therefore must not be distributed more widely than to the individual and the Chief Education Officer. The only exception to this is that the Senior Chief Inspector who has ultimate responsibility for the Professional Appraiser should be enabled to operate an impersonal sampling system to monitor the performance of the Professional Appraisers [Committee of Heads of Educational Institutions, 1986].

However, it can be immediately seen that this, too, is merely another form of feedback. A roving band of appraisers, changing in composition, appraising as infrequently as with a three-year interval will have little effect on the quality of our schools.

Very much closer to a model offering true appraisal with its essential ingredient of managerial responsibility for the appraiser's performance is one proposed by Lyn Jones (1983). This he calls the Control Model and it indicates management control of headteachers being narrowed down to two sources, the governing body and the CEO. Close as this is to an operational reality it still raises the following objections:

1. Most CEOs could not directly exercise management appraisal over all headteachers in their organization. Many education authorities have over fifty secondary headteachers alone, in addition to primary and tertiary heads. It would inevitably be necessary for the CEOs to delegate management and appraisal of heads to a nominee, presumably with a line-management relationship between CEO and headteacher. This is the role which could be filled by the school superintendent.
2. Reservations about the efficacy of governing bodies as appraisers of headteachers have already been expressed.
3. No headteacher should be made accountable to two sources simultaneously. To make an appraisal system effective either the governing body, through a nominee, accepts management and appraisal responsibility for the head or these functions are exercised through the CEO. The headteacher who is double-managed is left with the stress of conflicting pressures from his or her two managerial sources or with the prospect of playing-off one source against the other. I see no other possible effective manager and appraiser of the headteacher than an Anglicized version of the role of the US school superintendent.

WHAT WOULD BE THE ROLE OF A SCHOOL SUPERINTENDENT?

The school superintendent completes the chain of accountability from electorate to classroom teacher. The superintendent fills the missing link (see Figure 8) which makes the headteacher accountable to society.

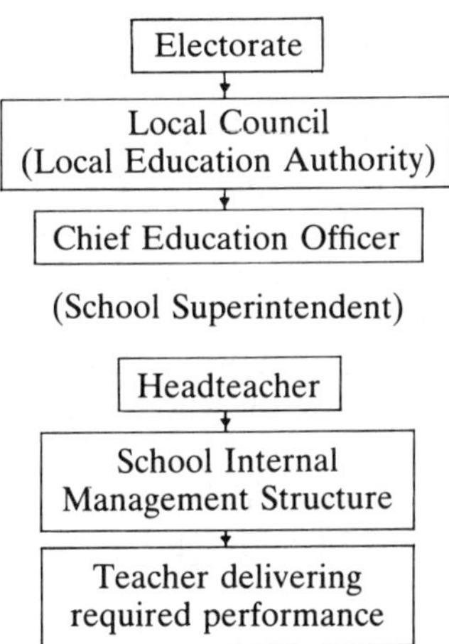

Figure 8 The missing link in headteacher accountability

The school superintendent accepts management responsibility for the performance of the headteacher. This involves appraising performance in the basic task, setting and appraising targets and exercising a day-to-day management relationship. Headteachers as well as teachers should be given an analyzed job description, be answerable to a clearly indicated manager using undisputed criteria for assessment and accepted performance standards supported by annual reviews. Any head who failed, at this annual review, to achieve the agreed performance standards should be asked to account for the failure, and the fault for lack of achievement should be clearly and fairly traced. A failure to achieve a target might be due to poor performance on the part of the headteacher or the staff. But it could also be due to lack of provision of resources of staffing on the part of the local authority. Perhaps, too optimistic a target was set and it might be necessary for the school catchment area to adjust itself to lower educational expectations. Whatever the cause of failure to meet expected standards, Headteacher appraisal by a managing superintendent could encourage its early identification and remedy. No head should fear that his or her acknowledged responsibility for managing the school is being challenged. Being accountable to a school superintendent will relieve the pressure on many headteachers not only by appraising last year's performance but by clearly identifying what is implied and expected for next year.

The school superintendent provides a promotion opportunity for headteachers. At present most headteachers remain in the first post to which they are promoted, although a proportion of them seek second headships. Without the benefit of a manager, effective headteachers have to be self-motivating to maintain a high level of enthusiasm, efficiency and efficacy. Few are able to achieve this state of continued self-development. Often appointed at about 40 years of age, a headteacher has the next 20 to 25 years ahead with little prospect of promotion except to another headship. This task of recharging one's motivation is a real problem which is seldom acknowledged, yet many headteachers feel the need for a fresh challenge. It is the root of the problem of some of our poorly performing schools. The problem should be acknowledged, examined and treated. It would be to a large extent eased by creating the post of school superintendent to which effective heads could aspire, or by whom their performance would be managed.

The school superintendent would have other administrative and advisory functions. He or she need not add yet another tier to the educational management hierarchy. There are practical, operating benefits to be gained from combining some functions of the adviser (support, inspection, training, etc.) with the Education Administration Service (administration, financing, resourcing, forecasting, etc.) and adding these to the executive management and appraisal functions of the school superintendent. In that combined post, experience of the role of headteacher would be invaluable. Such an overlap would reduce the distinction between career avenues which now exists in education and encourage greater understanding of the total education service task.

School superintendents, by appraising headteachers, set teachers an example. The Suffolk research report (1985) presents the reaction of an American teacher to the prospect of a teacher-appraisal system which did not contain provision for the appraisal of heads. 'It sure as hell would lack credibility if the principals and superintendents weren't evauated,' he said. If successful appraisal systems require commitment from the top of an organization, then the best way for a head to establish commitment is to set the pace and lead the change. The head has a strong influence on the tone of staff relationships. He or she can set standards of openness and positive confrontation and can find the example quickly identified and staff behaviour adjusted accordingly. In short, an appraised head is much more likely to develop an appropriate school ethos for the appraisal of staff.

THE BASIC TASK OF THE HEADTEACHER

The essential accountability analysis of headship must include:

1. A basic-task description for headteachers
2. A clearly defined manager responsible for the headteacher's performance and obliged to appraise performance regularly
3. A system of target setting with the headteacher's manager
4. A school to manage which in turn has a line-management structure leading ultimately to the headteacher, with a clearly indicated manager for every member of staff
5. Management training in key skills such as appraisal and leadership

The basic task of a headteacher can be expressed as principal accountabilities similar to what is done for all other staff. Most heads accept that they are responsible for everything which happens on the school premises, but this is an impossible and imprecise task. Headteachers surely should be given an analyzed job description. The job description, available in very few LEAs would help in the identification of the headteacher's principal accountabilities. The DES-funded POST project of the Open University undertaken by Colin Morgan and Valerie Hall found in their visits to 55 LEAs and a survey by questionnaire of a further 26 LEAs only one LEA which had a written description of the head's job (Morgan, Hall and Mackay, 1983). Such descriptions are widely used in the USA and an example is included as Document A at the end of this chapter. A proposal for the headteacher principal accountabilities would cover the areas of: ethos and aims; planning and control; review and improvement of performance; appointment and development of staff; and communication and relationships. Let us examine in detail these five principal accountabilities.

ETHOS AND AIMS

Create and maintain the appropriate ethos, aims, structures and curricula to maximize the potential of pupils for the good of themselves and of the community.

1. Create and maintain a school ethos with a suitable material intellectual, moral, spiritual and emotional environment.
2. Set up school aims and annual targets.
3. Create and maintain a system of pastoral care to support pupil development.
4. Create and maintain subject syllabuses appropriate to the age aptitude and ability of pupils, which fall within the policy of the LEA and which prepare pupils for appropriate external examinations.

PLANNING AND CONTROL

Plan the effective use of the resources of the school in relation to forecast pupil intakes and control the use of resources towards the stated aims and targets of the school.

1. Prepare realistic annual and five-year plans for the school based upon forecast pupil-intakes and likely curricular developments and cost these in school resources.
2. Set up suitable management and control systems to ensure achievement of aims and targets and for the proper accounting and control of resource use.

REVIEW AND IMPROVEMENT OF PERFORMANCE

Review and appraise the performance of the school, its staff teams and individual teachers towards the achievement of agreed school aims and targets.

1. Review school and departmental performance at least annually and produce appropriate records and reports on progress for staff, parents, governors, LEA and the local community.
2. Devise and maintain systems for the review and improvement of teacher performance and develop a positive staff attitude towards improvement.

3. Devise and maintain systems for the review and improvement of pupil performance and develop a positive staff and pupil attitude towards improvement.
4. Devise and maintain systems to maintain school buildings and grounds and develop a positive attitude towards improving the school environment.

APPOINTMENT AND DEVELOPMENT OF STAFF

Recruit and allocate roles and responsibilities to staff in such a way that the aims and targets of the school are achieved. Set an example in team management with the senior staff team.
1. Make successful appointments to the staff in accordance with agreed school plans.
2. Set up an organizational structure, using scale points to meet the needs of the school.
3. Motivate, control and facilitate the work of the senior management team, developing their skills by example and other stimuli.

COMMUNICATION AND RELATIONSHIPS

Develop and maintain effective communication and relationships with pupils, staff, parents, and with all bodies and agencies which serve the school to convey the progress of the school towards its aims.
1. Devise and maintain a system of personal, departmental and staff meetings and ensure feedback on target achievement at all levels.
2. Devise and maintain systems of in-school communication with pupils.
3. Devise and maintain systems of communication with parents on their children and on school matters generally.
4. Ensure that the governing body, local community and local media receive appropriate information on school matters.
5. Maintain an effective liaison with the LEA through its school superintendent, administrative officers and advisers.
6. Maintain an effective liaison with representatives of local industry and commerce and other schools and colleges.

SOURCES OF INFORMATION IN HEADTEACHER APPRAISAL

How can the school superintendent and headteacher obtain information on which to base an appraisal of the head's performance? Suggested sources are: a self-appraisal report from the headteacher; reports and surveys made to the school superintendent and the headteacher, jointly; and observation visits made by the school superintendent to the school.

A SELF-APPRAISAL REPORT FROM THE HEADTEACHER

Each headteacher should have the opportunity of contributing to his or her own appraisal. The design of the report could be left to the headteacher but it may be advisable to give some guidance on the expected content. A chronological approach is simplest, requiring the head to express his or her opinion on the performance of the basic task and of targets set last year, then to look forward to those proposed for the year ahead and finally to propose long-term targets. Other LEAs may wish to adapt the relevant sections of their self-evaluation documents. The Oxfordshire County Council Education Department Self-evaluation document, for example, asks the headteacher to contemplate the headteacher's role under the headings of: time; objectives and organization; staffing; and external relations.

The document sets questions for the headteacher to answer such as: How much time do I spend on administration and meetings in school? What do I see as the priorities for the school in the next term/year/five years? Do staff feel I am interested in their professional and their personal welfare and how do I express that interest? Have I satisfied myself that parents know to whom they can turn for help and that it will be forthcoming?

Clearly each LEA will decide upon the amount of direction it intends to give its headteachers in the form of self-appraisal report required.

Good feedback comes from people who work closest with you and know you best. For the headteacher this intimate knowledge belongs to his or her deputies or to the other members of the senior management team. Where the relationship between head and deputy has been built on mutual respect it may be possible for the deputy to give frequent performance feedback directly and personally to the head, looking for the good things being done but not avoiding the negatives. In many instances, however, open and honest comment on the head's performance by the deputy will not be thought possible. The relationship between the two colleagues will have developed in such a way that feedback would cause embarrassment or resentment. In such cases it may be possible for the members of the senior management team to complete a simple areas-for-improvement questionnaire, indicating strong and weaker areas in a headteacher's performance from the viewpoint of the deputy. An example of such a questionnaire is given at the end of this chapter as Document B.

The completed questionnaires would remain confidential to the headteacher, giving feedback which was intended to help his or her self-appraisal. It is not a 'snitch' system in which a deputy is appraising the performance of a headteacher and passing that appraisal on to the LEA.

For some schools, however, even the areas-for-improvement questionnaire might be unsuitable. A more sophisticated instrument such as the headteacher-feedback questionnaire may be more acceptable, especially if each member of the senior management team completes a copy and the head is given a composite analysis of how his or her performance is seen by the deputies. Replies to the questionnaire should be analyzed using the key. Both questionnaire and key are given in Document C at the end of this chapter. The replies can make the head aware of general areas where a team of colleagues believes his or her performance is good or bad.

How the information is used is once again the choice of the head. It is an immensely valuable form of feedback. It will not be discarded or resented except by the immature, and it can, like all forms of feedback, create awareness and present the opportunity for self-improvement.

Other feedback forms to help the headteacher in the task of self-appraisal could come from using listening skills effectively in the many staff interview situations. Appraisal interviews with the senior staff, second-tier interviews with teachers, exit interviews with staff who are leaving, grievance interviews, disciplinary interviews, any of these could provide valuable self-appraisal information for the head who is willing to listen and reflect on it.

A third source of information for the headteacher seeking self-appraisal information can be set up by using agreed self-monitoring devices. These are a form of target with objective performance standards agreed with the school superintendent. For example, the head may target to increase the number of review meetings with department heads by 50% or to create a new system to review pupil progress. Such objective criteria once established will be useful to the headteacher in reviewing his or her own performance.

There is no finite list of possible sources of feedback. The key to success lies in the attitude of mind which seeks to solicit feedback, to evaluate it and to act upon it.

REPORTS AND SURVEYS MADE TO THE SCHOOL SUPERINTENDENT AND HEADTEACHER JOINTLY

Reports would be expected from representative groups such as the governing body, the advisory service and parents association, with the aim of giving feedback, positive and negative on the performance of the school and the headteacher. When necessary surveys could be made of the opinions of larger groups such as the degree of satisfaction of feeder schools or local employers or the customers of the school, the parents. Although the reports would in general address school performance, the headteacher and the appraiser would sift them for feedback on headteacher performance.

OBSERVATION VISITS

The school superintendent would have the right and the duty to visit the school, talk to the head, staff and pupils and use the practice of 'management by walking about' (MBWA), discussed earlier, to form his or her appraisal of the performance of both headteacher and school.

TARGETS

Just as teachers in the school set personal targets so too would the head. Using the performance criteria described in earlier chapters the head and superintendent would agree on target achievement and from that rationalize further action.

Such a system as has been described would not only formalize certain important avenues of feedback but even more importantly would leave the head with a professional, experienced and skilled appraiser who would be fully responsible for the headteacher's performance.

SAMPLE DOCUMENTS

DOCUMENT A: HARDING SCHOOL DISTRICT ADMINISTRATIVE JOB DESCRIPTION

POSITION TITLE

Principal, Harding High School

QUALIFICATIONS

Hold a valid State Secondary School Principal's Certificate or be eligible to receive certification.

Hold a Masters' Degree in Administration.

Have a previous public-school administrative experience.

Have a minimum of three years' successful teaching experience at the secondary-school level.

Show evidence of an understanding of the 'learning process' and its implications on curriculum development.

Be able to develop a positive rapport and working relationship with professional and nonprofessional staff.

EMPLOYMENT TERMS (NUMBER OF MONTHS, ETC.)

12-month contract.

Salary and fringe benefits as per adopted schedule by the Harding Administrative Association and the school directors.

ORGANIZATIONAL LEVEL (REPORTING LEVEL)

The principal of Harding High School is the professional leader and chief administrator of the school and the Vo-Tech Center. He/she is in charge and has line authority over all personnel in the building — teachers, clerks, custodians and students. He/she is responsible to the superintendent for the total operation of the school and for organizing, administering, supervising and coordinating all the activities of the school and the coordination of all services in the building.

PRIMARY JOB FUNCTIONS

The principal shall administer and supervise his/her school in accordance with such policies, rules, and regulations as the superintendent and board of school directors may prescribe. He/she shall advise and keep the superintendent informed of all matters pertaining to the foregoing functions and perform such other duties as the superintendent may assign. In the discharge of the foregoing responsibilities the principal is assisted by certain administrative and supervisory personnel to whom authority and responsibility is delegated.

MAJOR DUTIES AND RESPONSIBILITIES

1. Planning, directing, organizing and supervising the instructional program of the school. Specifically he/she serves as operational leader of instruction with major responsibility for curriculum development, coordination, improvement and evaluation.
2. Planning, directing and supervising procedures and policies for the operation of the library and instructional materials and resources.
3. Planning and directing procedures for the school participating in special projects and events in conjunction with the school system, the community and other organizations. Planning and directing continuing programs for interpreting the school to pupils, parents, community organizations and other interested and/or affected persons or groups.
4. Planning, directing, promoting and supervising procedures for the organization and supervision of athletic and nonathletic student activities.
5. Develop and administer plans and procedures for the orientation, in-service training, supervision and evaluation of staff members; making recommendations to the superintendent on the selection, assignment, retention, promotion and dismissal of personnel.
6. Plan, direct, and supervise budget preparation activities, administer the approved budget, coordinate the school's budget procedures and policies with those of the superintendent's office.
7. Plan, direct, supervise and administer procedures for the use and rental of the building by community or outside groups according to established policies.
8. Planning, supervising, and administering the coordination of the school's maintenance procedures with the director of physical plant for the Harding School District.
9. Coordinate with the Vo-Tech director to establish and maintain close and cooperative working relationships with administrators and schools served in the area by the Harding Vo-Tech Center.
10. In conjunction with the director of pupil personnel services and special education programs, the principal will direct and supervise the activities designated as pupil personnel services, special education and federal programs.

CRITERIA FOR EVALUATION: (WHO WILL EVALUATE?)

The superintendent will evaluate the principal based on the performance of the job specifications and make recommendations to the board of school directors for employment. The principal's contract shall be renewed on an annual basis.

DOCUMENT B: AREAS FOR IMPROVEMENT

You can help your head become even more effective by suggesting those areas which need attention. Where do you think your head should put his/her efforts to improve? The following ten categories describe the head's job. For each category, indicate whether you feel your head should improve in performance. Mark each category as you feel is appropriate.

Category	Yes, significant improvement should be made	Yes, some improvement should be made	No, current performance is effective
Development providing his/her people with opportunities to develop their skills and knowledge	1 — Yes	2 — Some	3 — No
Motivation stimulating his/her people to achieve high levels of performance	1 — Yes	2 — Some	3 — No
Recognition acknowledging his/her people based on their performance	1 — Yes	2 — Some	3 — No
Consideration showing respect and concern for his/her people	1 — Yes	2 — Some	3 — No
Communication furthering two-way communication and understanding with his/her people	1 — Yes	2 — Some	3 — No
Decision making analyzing problems and selecting solutions	1 — Yes	2 — Some	3 — No
Planning developing work plans and objectives	1 — Yes	2 — Some	3 — No

Organization and control arranging and monitoring the unit's work effectively	1 — Yes	2 — Some	3 — No
Delegation giving responsibility, authority and autonomy to his/her people	1 — Yes	2 — Some	3 — No
Work facilitation providing resources (tools, knowledge, etc.) to help his/her people get the job done	1 — Yes	2 — Some	3 — No

DOCUMENT C: HEADTEACHER FEEDBACK FROM A DEPUTY HEAD

Please indicate your degree of satisfaction by putting the appropriate number in the corresponding box on the answer form

5 = Very satisfied
4 = Satisfied
3 = Neither satisfied nor dissatisfied
2 = Dissatisfied
1 = Very dissatisfied

How far do you feel your head carries out these functions in relation to you. Please indicate your degree of satisfaction with his/her performance:

1. Helps me to prepare for greater responsibility in the future.
2. Creates a climate that encourages excellence.
3. Is fair in evaluating my achievements.
4. Is good at analyzing problems.
5. Plans the work of the school well in advance.
6. Keeps a careful eye on as much of the school as possible.
7. Gives me enough freedom to do my job.
8. Helps me get the finance, staff or other resources to do my job.
9. Helps me to develop the skills needed in my present post.
10. Encourages me on the more difficult task in my present post.
11. Recognizes my contributions at appropriate times.
12. Keeps any promises or fulfils the commitments made to me.
13. Guides me by discussing my work openly and freely.
14. Considers the likely effects before he or she makes a decision.
15. Makes my job clear to me, and explains how I will be judged in it.
16. Organizes well his or her own work and where appropriate, that of others.
17. Gives me sufficient authority to make decisions and to implement them.

18. Is available for help and advice when I meet a problem I wish to talk through.
19. Encourages me by his or her own good example.
20. Shows me that he or she has trust and confidence in me.
21. Is willing to understand my point of view in any problem.
22. Is willing to make himself or herself available to me when this is needed.
23. Sets realistic aims for the school, which are possible for us to achieve.
24. Encourages departmental, pastoral or management teams to work together.
25. Is willing to delegate responsibility to senior staff.
26. Discusses my career plans and ambitions with me at least annually.
27. Detects and acknowledges good work.
28. Is willing to back me up when I need support.
29. Is willing to explain the reasons for his or her decision or action.
30. When under pressure or other forms of stress he or she still makes good decisions.
31. Is fair in the loading of tasks on senior staff.
32. Is good at managing meetings with staff or other groups.
33. Is helpful when I need assistance in sorting out school problems.
34. Helps me improve my performance.
35. Stresses the need to achieve any aims or targets set for me.
36. Discusses my performance with me rationally at reasonable intervals.
37. Actually cares about my opinions and ideas on school matters.
38. Creates occasions for communication with me.
39. Accepts the responsibility for his or her own decisions.
40. Makes successful appointments to the staff.
41. Gives me the opportunity to make decisions on my own.
42. Uses his or her experience and knowledge to help me in my work.
43. Encourages me to plan my career.
44. Gives me feedback at the appropriate time on how I am doing my job.
45. Listens to me when I have something to say.
46. Keeps me informed about things which could affect me and my job.
47. Makes his or her decisions without undue delay.
48. Tackles the problem of poor performance by any member of staff as appropriate.
49. Allows me to develop my own way of doing the job I have been given.
50. Plans and arranges appropriate training for me to enable me to do my present job.

HEADTEACHER FEEDBACK QUESTIONNAIRE

To be completed by deputy headteacher.
Write feedback number in box below appropriate question number.

A	B	C	D	E	F	G	H	I	J
1	2	3	—	—	4	5	6	7	8
9	10	11	12	13	14	15	16	17	18
—	19	20	21	22	—	23	24	25	—
26	—	27	28	29	30	31	32	—	33
34	35	36	37	38	39	40	—	41	42
43	44	—	45	46	47	—	48	49	50

HEADTEACHER FEEDBACK QUESTIONNAIRE

Reply Analysis

Total the feedback numbers in each column. Columns indicate the following areas of headteacher performance as experienced by the deputy head.

A. Development of the deputy by the head
B. Motivation of the deputy by the head
C. Recognition of contribution of the deputy by the head
D. Consideration for the deputy as an individual by the head
E. Communication with the deputy by the head
F. Decision making by the head
G. Organization and control of staff by the head
H. Organization and control of staff by the head
I. Delegation by head to the deputy and close colleagues
J. Head facilities the work of the deputy

Maximum score: 25 in each area of performance.
Use the column scores to assess strengths and weakness in performance areas.

9 THE MANAGEMENT CONTROL OF SCHOOLS BY LEAs

The major problems for the management control of schools arise because of the difficulty in identifying the objectives of schools compared with those of industrial firms. School objectives are usually self-selected purposes based on some in-house variation of a generic aim to provide a sound education by making the best possible use of the available resources. The problem is exacerbated because of the compound and subjective nature of the concept of a sound education. It is also vague and is less measurable than the key commercial objective of profit making. This absence of a single measure has many implications for decision making in schools.

Firstly, in the absence of the profit measure or of any other single objective measure of success there is no single criterion that can be used in evaluating proposed courses of action either in schools or on behalf of schools. Decision making therefore becomes a much more subjective and professionally rooted activity and more difficult for the nonprofessional to challenge.

Secondly, schools find it almost impossible to measure output. If pseudo-objective criteria such as external-examination results were to be used alone to assess the success of a school they would not necessarily be a measure of achievement of the total objective of the school and could in fact encourage schools to distort that real purpose to achieve those objectives which are more easily measurable.

An historical parallel may be seen in 'payment by results' set up in the nineteenth century under the Revision Code of 1862. Having examination passes as the objective resulted as it so often does in excessive pressure to produce results to meet what were in effect the school's performance criteria. It demoralized teachers; their quality declined. Teacher hostility towards inspectors increased as did attempts to hoodwink them by making children learn by heart concepts which it was claimed they understood.

Kay Shuttleworth, Education Secretary said of that objective-setting exercise, 'The Revised Code has constructed nothing: It has only pulled down.' Clearly there are dangers in seeking only those performance criteria which are objective.

The problem of resource allocation to schools is another of the more difficult aspects of management control of schools for LEAs. How much of each resource should they allocate to a school to produce a certain quality of education? If a given amount of resources fails to produce this quality of education, is this due to inadequate resourcing, to incompetent misuse of the resource within the school or to misdirected use of the resources towards an educational aim the LEA does not endorse?

The lack of relationship between cost and product in schools is another factor making it difficult to assess school effectiveness. For example, it is not easy to present a case for an increase or decrease in staffing because one cannot judge the marginal change which will occur in performance as one or more teacher is added to the school establishment. This creates a conflict of judgement criteria between effective resource utilization (to meet the objective of a good education) and efficient resource utilization (to reduce costs).

Another missing comparison is that of market forces in many decision-making areas in schools. Decisions therefore have to be made according to the best judgements of senior and middle management, very much in isolation and potentially with less accuracy.

Nor is it easy to measure school success in financial terms. The only real financial target a school has is not to overspend its budget and to break even over the relevant accounting period, rendering as much service as possible with a given amount of resource. This may be the closest a school can come to having a financially linked target.

A final management problem for the control of schools by the LEA is that their heads have little knowledge or experience of management-control practices such as cost accounting, budgeting and programming. Few schools would, for example, be able to implement such techniques as critical path-analysis or zero-based budgeting. In many organizations, the problem is not so much the wrong strategy as difficulty in securing its effective execution. Inadequate systems, ill-equipped or poorly motivated staff and an inappropriate managerial style can frustrate any school's best laid plans.

But problems of management by the LEA are not all one way. Schools too experience difficulty in being subject to an LEA and elected representative control. Firstly, there may be a reversal between objectives and constraints as we travel from top to bottom of the educational service. At one end we have the local council with the public duty to keep the budget lean and rates down and at the other end we have headteachers trying to secure as large a budget as they can for their schools. The same conflict exists in output. The school tries to provide the best possible service, the local council may come closer to a target of the minimum acceptable level of service or at least the minimum amount of education service it can offer without public outcry.

If 'he who pays the piper calls the tune' and control of schools is seen as being exercised by the county council or other body representing the electorate, then schools can expect a further problem. Elected bodies sometimes feel the need to be seen by the electorate as efficient managers on some occasions and as providers of an outstanding service on others, and this can create short-term changes of plans and programmes which may be to the detriment of the long-run objectives of the school.

THE WAY AHEAD

Where should we begin if we are to introduce staff performance appraisal into our schools? The first step has to be to identify our objectives. Without clear objectives performance appraisal is a waste of time. What are the primary objectives of education? of schools? Within each school what is expected of each department? each teacher? In short where are we going and what contribution is expected from each of us to achieve that destination?

Setting aims and objectives for a school as required by the 1980 Education Act is not sufficient to ensure success. Writing *Blackpool* on a bus will not ensure that town as its destination.

It is abundantly clear that we cannot quickly set up some objectives for an enterprise and then proceed on the assumption that they will be meaningful guides to action. However, we do know that objectives

> . . . need not begin with the broad grand design of the enterprise, but all objectives in the hierarchy should be consistent with it;
> . . . should make the people in the enterprise reach a bit;
> . . . should be realistic in terms of (a) the internal resources of the enterprise, and (b) the external opportunities, threats, and constraints;
> . . . should take into account the creative conception of a range of alternatives and the relative effectiveness and cost of each;
> . . . should be known to each person so that he understands the goals of his own work and how they relate to the broader objectives of the total enterprise;
> . . . should be periodically reconsidered and redefined, not only to take account of changing conditions but for the salutary effect of rethinking the aims of organizational activities.

> Objectives, properly developed and applied, can tell us in what paths, new and old, our total undertakings should be moving. They can guide both the day-to-day activities and the personal development of individuals in an organization. If we in management can clarify the objectives of our undertakings by even a small amount, we can greatly increase the effectiveness and efficiency of our business [Granger, 1964].

This applies no less to educational establishments than to those of industry and commerce: clarify the objectives of schools.

Next we need to redesign the school accountability system. Specify within schools the levels of responsibility and establish who is responsible to whom. Use the concept of project and report for any work undertaken outside the responsibility area of the teacher's appraiser, in which there is feedback on the teacher's performance to that appraiser from the person responsible for the project. I do not believe that creating that accountability structure will be a difficult task. Much more difficult to achieve will be making the headteacher accountable to a manager who can give day-to-day advice as well as meaningful annual appraisals. This should be the task of a school superintendent, accountable to the CEO for the performance of those headteachers within the superintendent's span of control. This implies greater active involvement from LEAs through not only the local inspectorate and governing boards but the revolutionary new step of the creation of the post of school superintendent to manage headteacher's performances, clarify the objectives, separate desirable from essential objectives, emphasize coordination and communication, and identify measures of efficiency and efficacy which do not distort the role which society depends upon schools to fulfil.

We must support this new accountability structure with:

- More headteacher involvement in performance evaluation and systems' improvement, and clear rejection by the education service of poor performance.
- Link the headteachers career development to improved school performance by continuing the promotion ladder via the superintendent route.
- Establish better rewards for the school for good housekeeping and good management including wider control of the total school budget and the retention of funds 'saved' for service improvement.
- The relationship between costs and service should be identified wherever possible in special areas, and a zero-based budget review should be undertaken every five years.
- Place greater emphasis on the measure of output. Use cost and other comparisons within and between schools to identify best practices.

I see no alternative but that we plan, train and develop for a behavioural change in those managing schools towards: a better identification of targets; better organizational design; and better techniques of management to provide better control, ensuring that senior and middle management in schools will act to balance efficiency and efficacy. Unless we can encourage headteachers and those who will manage them to develop skills of management control through better understanding and training, then any technical improvements in our service are likely to have little real impact. We also need both awareness courses and skills training in performance appraisal for all staff in schools. Teachers, from the experienced to the trainee, need to know how they should prepare for appraisal, what is expected of them during appraisal interviews and what the consequences are of being appraised. Appraisers need to acquire the skills of appraisal from which can develop both commitment to the process and the confidence to handle an appraisal in a way that gives teachers reassurance.

Lastly, there will be need to reconsider resources allocated to teacher development. A large percentage of the time, finance, space, effort and expertise required to help teachers develop will increasingly come from within schools in the form of on-the-job training. A further large percentage of the training resources may need to be made much more directly available to schools to meet needs they have identified through their appraisal systems. University and college in-service departments may need to be starved of resources for some of their provider-initiated courses in order that user- and purchaser-initiated needs can be met. Industrial companies in the past faced this conflict of academic management versus practical management; of award-bearing, long courses versus shorter, more frequently skills-based units. Those companies have resolved it heavily in favour of practical, regular short courses led by experienced managers in their own in-house management development centres. Any LEA could do the same and in doing so would more effectively control and direct its training resources towards meeting operating needs.

Helping teachers identify areas for personal and professional development is only half the battle. Offering effective training support is the other half.

How do these suggestions form a coordinated plan to help our schools? Firstly, identification of the purposes of schools will allow each school to have a clearer view of its role, its objectives and so to review its success. Better training in measuring school inputs and outputs will give society the means of controlling its schools and, together with clearer objectives, lead to a better use of school resources.

For staff, task clarification, target setting and appraisal will, together with improved skills through better training and development, lead to improved teacher performance. Effective use of resources, by a well-motivated and better trained teacher force, will mean an improved school performance towards the agreed purposes of a school. In successful schools:

- Objectives are known and shared by all staff not only the top management of the school.
- If things go wrong teachers do not hide their mistakes and problems but expect to discuss and solve them.
- Both personal and professional needs are discussed.
- Decisions are taken near the point of implementation.
- The head does not try to control all decisions but respects the judgement of others.
- Teachers do not feel alone, but rather part of a team lead by the appraiser but in which there is much sharing of responsibility.
- Feedback on performance and discussion of progress are standard practice. Poor performance is identified and tackled.
- There is an order and a structure to the school but teachers expect to innovate to meet changing circumstances and opportunities.

Schools such as these would be providing the best possible environment in which young pupils and students could help to prepare themselves for life in the twenty-first century.

APPENDIX I

THE BASIC TASK: PRINCIPAL AND DETAILED ACCOUNTABILITIES FOR THE TEACHER

The principal accountabilities for the teacher in the basic task are separated into five major sections: pastoral; teaching; personal skills development; departmental and school community; and administration. Each section is subdivided into its main accountabilities which are then detailed; some incorporate further recommendations where relevant.

The pastoral section is comprised of: knowledge of every child as an individual, realization of the significance of phrase *in loco parentis*; running tutor group to create a personal and group relationship; reporting to parents; contributing to development as a tutor; contributing to effective house organization; school policy; and identification of problems encountered by members of the tutor group.

The teaching section contains: preparation of lessons; classroom management including safety of pupils; marking of class and homework; and evaluation of pupils' achievements, awareness of their abilities, problems and personalities.

In personal-skills development, the main areas are: subject-related skills; professional-skills development; development of others; deputizing and sharing responsibilities; and motivation of pupils.

The section on departmental and school community involves: participation in extracurricular activities; contribution to morale; development of professional attitude, appearance, and conduct; contribution towards an effective department; attendance at and contribution to departmental meetings; and contribution to the departmental stock of teaching materials and to syllabus review.

Administration is subdivided into: department records; detentions; and school duties.

PASTORAL

1.1 *KNOW AND UNDERSTAND EACH CHILD AS AN INDIVIDUAL*

- Remember each teacher's role in **in loco parentis**.
- Acquire and maintain a thorough knowledge of each pupil, and its background, in the group.
- Form a professional, objective and caring relationship with each child exercising general oversight of academic and social development.
- Effectively identify strengths, talents, ambitions and endeavour to extend each individual in these areas.
- Effectively identify any problems being experienced by an individual in the group.
- Recommend and contribute to effective plans of action to overcome problems, weaknesses, identified in individuals in the group by subject teachers and others.
- Let pupils know you are available for help and discussion so that they feel confident and trust you and your judgement.
- Thoroughly study all records of pupils joining your group.
- Keep your tutor file up to date — using it as a day-to-day log of each individual's achievements and development. Make notes **at the time** to assist later in report writing etc.
- Keep each individual's records up to date as fully as possible.
- Use your professional skills as a teacher to help each individual but **know** when to refer a problem — when other skills are needed.
- Encourage initiative and independence, ensuring each individual is given opportunity to lead, direct and organize activities — the scale and scope of which will vary with the age and ability of the individual concerned.
- Keep all pastoral deadlines in the interest of each individual pupil's welfare.

1.2 *RUNNING A TUTOR GROUP*

- Be present for the full period of registration, assembly or other appropriate meeting between 9.00 and 9.30 a.m.
- Keep an accurate register of attendance with strict adherence to school's procedure for register keeping. Draw the attention of the house head to 'patterns' of lateness/absence.
- Establish a sound routine — giving out information at the beginning of each session so as not to require settling the group more than once.

• Cover the topic areas in the pastoral-care section of the staff diary between dates suggested. Limit administration to taking the register only in tutor periods earmarked for these topics.
• Ensure confidentiality so that information is in possession of only those who need to have access. The responsibility to judge which information is confidential will be that of the head of house.
• Develop a personal relationship with each individual (see 1.1).
• Develop a group relationship with the group.
• Ensure homework diaries are checked regularly.
• Ensure optimum benefit for individuals is achieved.
• Through the fostering of a group relationship — make pupils aware of the requirements of others in the tutor group.

1.3 *REPORTING TO PARENTS*

• Establish and maintain a professional relationship with parents in close liaison with your house head.
• Reporting should be on time, accurate, and allowing adequate time for the parent to discuss points raised.
• Take a pride in the professional delivery of reports to parents on the appropriate evenings.
• Ensure follow-up action to reports is completed/implemented on the day of delivery or on the following day.
• Suggest the initiation of interim reports — collect and deliver as appropriate.
• Ensure your house head is aware of favourable and unfavourable comments from parents. These interviews are a valuable source of feedback for the school.

1.4 *CONTRIBUTE TO YOUR DEVELOPMENT AS A TUTOR*

• Consider your successes and failures at least termly and discuss these with your house head.
• Discuss with your house head any action necessary for resolving problems — academic/behaviour or social — experienced by individuals in your group (see 1.1).
• Keep all pastoral deadlines (see 1.1).
• Work with your house head in identifying areas of your professional performance in which you need more experience or need to improve.
• Notify your house head of any developments in house or pastoral policy you feel are needed.

1.5 *CONTRIBUTE TO EFFECTIVE HOUSE*

- Develop a group relationship and feeling of belonging to.
- Foster house spirit — pride of tutor and group in the house.
- Make pupils aware of the requirements of others in the house and society in general (see 1.2).
- Foster involvement in charity work of the house.
- Encourage house teams and become involved with or support them.
- Offer support and participation in house assemblies.
- Remember that you, your house head and deputy form a team and are mutually supportive.
- Keep all pastoral deadlines in the interest of each individual pupil's welfare (see 1.1) and in fairness to your colleagues.

1.6 *SCHOOL POLICY*

- Support and be seen by pupils to support school policy.
- Ensure the implementation of school policy within the tutor group, encouraging the achievements, aims and objectives of the school.
- Ensure that your house head is aware of favourable and unfavourable comments from parents. Interviews with parents are a valuable source of feedback for the school (see 1.3).

1.7 *IDENTIFICATION OF PROBLEMS*

- Effectively identify any problems being experienced by pupils in your tutorial group and recommend effective plan of action to your house head.
- Contribute to the solution of problems identified in your tutorial pupils by subject teachers.

TEACHING

2.1 *PREPARATION OF LESSONS*

To ensure that

- Resources needed are identified or booked or requested from reprographics or resources centre at least one week in advance.
- Programme/scheme is planned at least a term in advance and agreed with head of department.
- Lessons are adequately planned and documented in record book so that another teacher could take over in your absence.
- Adequate and appropriate use is made of visual aids, worksheets etc.
- Materials used are of high enough quality to add to department stock.
- Subject matter adequately fills timetable periods.

Further recommendations

- Define specific milestones and deadlines, documented in record book.
- Use record book to help prepare/repeat prototype lessons.
- Spend enough time researching subject to cover the syllabus adequately as judged by ability to answer related questions from the class etc.
- Discuss your approach to preparation with your head of department etc.
- Ensure that any visual aids you make are colourful, creative, imaginative, understandable, etc., and to a standard that you would like to be used by others.
- Review your use of visual aids, worksheets, etc. with head of department.

2.2 *CLASSROOM MANAGEMENT INCLUDING SAFETY OF PUPILS*

To ensure that

- All materials for each class are set up and ready on time.
- Each class starts and ends on time.
- Each lesson completed covers the intended subject matter.
- Your classroom is tidy and well set out.
- There is at least one display or exhibition of work in the classroom.
- There is no disruption of adjoining classes or disorder in the group.
- The safety of pupils in your class is foremost particularly when electrical equipment or specialized apparatus is used.

Further recommendations

- Generate high activity levels with good interaction.
- Create an interested and responsive class.
- Create a happy, positive atmosphere.
- Change displays, exhibitions on a regular basis.
- Recognize the contribution that each child is making.
- Know when to refer children to head of department, deputy, etc.
- Discuss your ability to provide discipline and control with other teachers and the head of department.
- Find out what your head of department thinks of your classroom techniques.

2.3 *MARKING AND HOMEWORK*

To ensure that

- Work is returned within one week.

- All marks are recorded in the mark book.
- Mark books are presented, up to date, by pay day.
- Homework is set in accordance with the timetable.
- In general homework set is related to classwork and that it constitutes a discrete unit of work.
- Internal examinations are set and made available on time.

Further recommendations

- Provide pupils with constructive and helpful comments on work as appropriate.
- Provide personal feedback to each pupil as appropriate.
- Look at other methods of marking and compare your own with other teachers.
- Look at other groups in the department to assess/compare standards.
- Analyze success/suitability of homework, etc. and note in record book for future reference.

2.4 *EVALUATION OF PUPILS' ACHIEVEMENTS, AWARENESS OF THEIR PROBLEMS AND PERSONALITIES*

- Strive and maintain and improve departmental standards and examination results.
- Enter children for the appropriate examinations consistent with their potential.
- Identify underachievers and gifted pupils and develop an appropriate action plan with head of department.
- Know the ability, attitude and background of each child in class.
- Provide the head of department with an accurate assessment of class ability.
- Provide constructive feedback to parents on each child's ability through reporting or interview systems of the school.

Further recommendations

- Ensure that the class is able to keep up with your programme of work or to modify it accordingly.
- Assess the standard of written/oral work against examination standards.
- Ensure that the class works together well as a group.
- Provide constructive input to tutors on difficulties, attitude, social skills, etc. and find out about problems experienced in other classes.

PERSONAL SKILLS DEVELOPMENT

3.1 *SUBJECT-RELATED SKILLS*

- Aim at the acquisition of at least one formal example of new subject skills each year, e.g., external course, syllabus development, etc.
- At the same time maintain your existing subject skill levels.

Further recommendations

- Research existing or new subject areas through private study on a regular basis.
- Take on new parts of the syllabus or new courses as appropriate to develop your own knowledge of the subject.
- Discuss your subject-related skills with your head of department, other teachers, etc.

3.2 *PROFESSIONAL SKILLS DEVELOPMENT*

- Consciously work at the development of skills such as communication, personal relationship, leadership, interviewing parents or pupils, creativity and the use of flair of judgement.
- Develop your ability in the fields of resources management, time management, personal organization.
- Work on at least one formal example of skills acquisition in this area, e.g., external course, intradepartmental course, etc.

Further recommendations

- Obtain feedback from the headmaster, head of department and other appropriate senior members of staff on the development of your professional skills, e.g., creativity, leadership, initiative, flair, judgement, sensitivity, time and resource management, communications, interviewing, etc.
- Agree an action plan to address areas where attention should be given to improving these skills.
- Understand other organizations and their roles and responsibilities in relation to professional development, e.g., Teachers Centre, county courses, university and polytechnic courses, the Open University, etc.

3.3 *DEVELOPMENT OF OTHERS*

- Provide feedback to head of department on the performance of junior colleagues working under your guidance, e.g., probationers, inexperienced teachers, etc.

- Accept responsibility for the professional development of student teachers under your supervision, giving guidance in planning, teaching techniques and in follow-up discussions.
- Link effectively with the tutor of any student-teacher allocated to you as necessary.

Further recommendations

- Spend time with junior colleagues to help them assess and improve their performance. Identify and help to overcome specific problems.
- Suggest ways in which others could be used most effectively to improve the efficiency of yourself or the department.

3.4 *DEPUTIZING AND SHARING RESPONSIBILITY*

- Stand in for senior colleagues as appropriate, effectively carrying out agreed tasks.
- Provide at least one example of involvement in department management or equivalent each year.

Further recommendations

- Suggest to head of department areas of responsibility that could be delegated to you or that you would like to be involved in.
- Discuss with head of department or head your effectiveness as a deputy/stand-in.
- Encourage junior colleagues to stand in for you, or to undertake some of your tasks. Provide constructive feedback to them on their performance.

3.5 *MOTIVATION OF PUPILS*

- Encourage each pupil to reach his/her full potential.
- Help to increase or maintain a pupil's confidence.

Further recommendations

- Introduce new/interesting ways of teaching your subject to ensure the involvement and enthusiasm of pupils (as judged by your own impression and observation of head of department, head, etc.).
- Discuss with the departmental head how best to find out what your classes think about your style through feedback from them, parents, etc.
- Analyze where appropriate the number of pupils selecting your subject as an option in the fourth year, from third year classes, to help with your research on motivation.

DEPARTMENTAL AND SCHOOL COMMUNITY

4.1 *PARTICIPATION IN EXTRACURRICULAR ACTIVITIES*

• Take a fair share of the long-term extracurricular activities of the department, e.g., clubs, societies, individual or small group support work.
• Take a fair share of the short-term extracurricular activity; share some of the work and prepare yourself to be able to lead a similar activity.
• Consider with the deputy head any gaps in the extracurricular provision of the school and offer to fill them.

4.2 *CONTRIBUTION TO MORALE*

• Notice signs in your colleagues which indicate over fatigue or overreaction, and help your head of department or give advice or practical assistance at such times.
• Help less experienced department members to improve their teaching, e.g., by inviting them to observe your lessons.
• Be willing to share teaching materials or give advice to colleagues.
• Be generous in thanks or praise for the help or good work of colleagues.

4.3 *PROFESSIONAL ATTITUDE, APPEARANCE, CONDUCT*

• Adopt a professional attitude in all relationships with colleagues, pupils, parents.
• Maintain professional dress and appearance at school.
• Maintain a high standard of professional conduct in all matters.

4.4 *CONTRIBUTE TO AN EFFECTIVE DEPARTMENT*

• Consider your 'successes' and 'failures' at least termly and discuss these with your head of department.
• Work with your head of department identifying areas of your professional work in which you need to gain further experience or to improve.
• Notify your head of department of any development in departmental policy you feel is needed.

4.5 *ATTENDANCE AT AND CONTRIBUTION TO DEPARTMENTAL MEETINGS*

• Attend all departmental meetings and contribute to their efficiency and efficacy.

• Prepare your contribution to all pupil-progress meetings.
• Meet with the tutor or house head to help resolve a problem any pupil is experiencing.

4.6 *CONTRIBUTE TO DEPARTMENT TEACHING MATERIAL STOCK AND TO SYLLABUS REVIEW*

• Know well the department's syllabus, organization, equipment.
• Make positive written suggestions about the continuing development of the department.
• Plan and accept responsibility for at least two 'long units' of work for the department (i.e., half-term normal in length) each year.
• Accept and execute at least two additional responsibilities each year, e.g., administration, stock, stationery, set lists, etc. within the department as agreed with the head of department.

ADMINISTRATION

5.1 *DEPARTMENT RECORDS*

To ensure that
• Record books are kept up to date and presented on time by pay day.
• Mark books are kept up to date and presented on time by pay day.
• Register check is made each lesson and used as an early warning system for absenteeism, difficulties, etc.
• Examination papers are prepared and available on time.
• Pupils are properly briefed on examination procedure.
• Examinations are marked according to departmental standards and timescale.
• Reports, annual and interim are written according to school procedure and available on time.
• Examination assessments (externals) are available on time, and with best possible degree of accuracy (e.g., within one grade).

Further recommendations

• Include in record book an analysis of suitability of lesson, details of materials (e.g., worksheets) used, suggestions for improvement.
• Discuss use of record and mark books with colleagues, head of department, etc. to find methods of improving, and with junior colleagues to provide advice.
• Provide individual comments on reports for each pupil, independent of other subjects or pupils.

• Discuss your assessments of examination potential with colleagues, head of department, etc. Review the accuracy of your past assessments to help define standards.

5.2 *DETENTIONS*

To ensure that
• Detentions are set with 24 hours' notice to pupil and parent.
• Detentions are accurately recorded.
• Detentions are carried out in accordance with handbook, with appropriate amount of extra work set.
• Work set is completed adequately or repeated.

Further recommendations

• Monitor number of detentions given to pupil, and report excessive amounts to tutor/head of department.
• Review your own use of detentions against school standards. Take action to avoid excessive numbers.
• Review with tutor if excessive detention given to individual pupil.

5.3 *DUTIES AND SCHOOL SUPPORT*

• Perform before school at break or after-school duties in accordance with rota. To be punctual and available to ensure proper order and discipline.
• Attend assembly, tutor meeting or department meeting on each day according to agreed 9.00–9.30 a.m. schedule.
• Be aware of the regulations regarding health and safety at work. Understand how to use safety equipment and procedures, and actions to take in an emergency. Ensure that parents are made aware of school rules and procedures.

APPENDIX II

ITEMS OF TASK DESCRIPTION WITH SELF-MONITORING APPRAISAL MEASURES

ITEMS	CRITERIA
DAILY SERVICES OF THE TIMETABLE	
To provide relief teachers, including external supply teachers, for all absent staff	(a) No classes without a teacher. (b) Relief notice displayed in staffroom by 9.30 a.m. without error
ARRANGEMENTS FOR EXAMINATIONS	
Ensure successful preparations for external examinations GCE (CSE through CSE examinations' secretary), City & Guilds and Pitmans	No errors in entries subjects or timing. Timetables issued by agreed dates to staff and pupils
Ensure accurate and timely completion of all returns and analyses related to examinations	All returns completed by stipulated dates and without error. An analysis of all school GCE and CSE results for the year to be ready by last Sunday of summer holidays each year.
CURRICULUM LIAISON WITH OTHER EDUCATIONAL ESTABLISHMENTS	
Primary schools (not transfer of new pupils) apart from early entrants	Visit all feeders at least twice per year in terms 1 and 2 (or once with a return visit from primary head).

ASSESSMENTS

Collection coordination and distribution of pupil assessments to parents	(a) Ensure assessments on all appropriate pupils collected by 3 weeks before agreed distribution date (b) Ensure assessment letters completed by distribution date (c) Ensure despatch of all assessments on agreed distribution date Distribution to all parents by deadline dates

APPENDIX III

A TWO-DAY TRAINING COURSE FOR TEACHER APPRAISERS

APPRAISAL: A COURSE FOR THOSE WHO CONDUCT APPRAISAL INTERVIEWS — LEADER'S GUIDE

9.00 INTRODUCTION
Welcome participants to the course.
If they don't know each other well, get them to introduce themselves very briefly.
Introduce yourself.
Explain that the course assumes no prior knowledge and that any person can be taught to conduct a good appraisal interview.
Resolve any problems or queries that trainees may have at this stage.
OH1 Go through the learning objectives for the course. These are:

OBJECTIVES

At the end of the course you should be able to:

- Appraise teacher performance against job requirements and standards
- Identify obstacles to satisfactory teacher performance
- Agree plans with the teacher that will improve short-term performance and contribute to the realization of career objectives

OH2 Explain how the two days will work, including the timetable.
Note that the timetable can vary depending on the amount of practical exercises and whether the video is used.

APPRAISAL INTERVIEWING: TWO DAYS

(Incorporating role-play sessions using video.)

Day 1

9.00	Introduction
9.30	FILM
10.00	Preparing for the interview
10.30	COFFEE
10.45	Structure of the interview
11.45	Specific interviewing skills
12.45	LUNCH
2.00	Video demo 1
2.30	Preparation for role plays
3.00	COFFEE
3.15	Role plays using CCTV
5.30	Finish

Day 2

9.00	Target setting and appraisal
10.15	COFFEE
10.30	Video demo 2
11.00	Preparation
11.30	Role plays using CCTV
12.15	LUNCH
1.30	Role plays using CCTV
3.00	COFFEE
3.15	Following the interview
3.45	Appraisal administration
4.30	Wind up
5.00	FINISH

OH3 Explain why we do appraisals.

THE PURPOSE OF APPRAISAL IS TO IMPROVE PERFORMANCE

At the appraisal we can plan to:

- Improve ability
- Increase motivation
- Remove other barriers to effective performance

Ask the group what the benefits of appraisal are. Write these up on the flipchart.

9.30 FILM: *How am I doing*?

10.00 PREPARING FOR AN APPRAISAL INTERVIEW

Ask the group what should be done to prepare for an appraisal. Write up on flip. Summarize by reading out the list in handout No. 1.

Ask group what factors influence someone's performance. Summarize by showing the interrelationship of factors as shown in handout No. 2.

FACTORS INFLUENCING PERFORMANCE
APTITUDE × LEARNING =
ABILITY × MOTIVATION =
INDIVIDUAL PERFORMANCE × ATTITUDE =
OVERALL CONTRIBUTION

10.30 COFFEE (15 mins)

10.45 STRUCTURE OF THE INTERVIEW

Four basic forms of work discussion

OH5 Explain the four types. Uncover the overhead slide as you go.

FOUR BASIC FORMS OF WORK DISCUSSION
DISCOVERY
PROBLEM SOLVING
ANNOUNCEMENT/DIRECTION
PERSUASION/NEGOTIATION

Appraisal is primarily a PROBLEM-SOLVING discussion. Consolidate by issuing handout No. 3.

Basic structure of all work discussions.

OH6 Explain the four stages, uncovering the overhead slide as you go. Consolidate by issuing handout No. 4

STRUCTURE OF ALL WORK DISCUSSIONS
CLIMATE OPENERS EXPLORATION CLOSURE

Outline for the appraisal interview. Introduce by issuing handout No. 5 Here you need to show how the structure for work discussions applies to the appraisal interview in particular. Go through each stage in depth, encouraging discussions and making sure each trainee understands.

OH7 Use the overhead slide to summarize.

OUTLINE FOR THE APPRAISAL INTERVIEW

CLIMATE
OPENERS
EXPLORATION

- PERFORMANCE REVIEW

• PERFORMANCE ANALYSIS
• INDIVIDUAL NEEDS AND ASPIRATIONS
• FUTURE JOB REQUIREMENTS
CLOSURE
70% APPRAISEE/30% APPRAISER

Work discussion openers.
Explain the idea behind openers — as described in handout No. 6.
OH8 Use the overhead slide to show the concept of theme lines creating the 'room' and the cue line opening the 'door' for the interviewee.

THEME LINES
DEFINE THE BOUNDARIES OF THE DISCUSSION

CUE LINES
OPEN THE DOOR FOR THE OTHER PERSON

Appraisal interview openers
Read out the examples from handout No. 6. Then get trainees to individually prepare their own examples of openers.
11.45 SPECIFIC INTERVIEWING SKILLS
1. Questioning skills
Follow the format in the handout. Explain the difference between direct and open questions. Get them to write an example and check these.
2. Listening skills
OH9 Explain each of the five techniques uncovering the overhead slide as you go. Give as many examples as are necessary to ensure understanding. Consolidate by using handout No. 7.

LISTENING
SILENCE ACKNOWLEDGEMENTS DOOR OPENERS/PRODS
PARAPHRASING REFLECTING FEELINGS

3. Giving feedback
OH10 Explain using the overhead slide. Read the examples in the handout No. 8. Add others of your own if necessary.

EFFECTIVE FEEDBACK IS:
DESCRIPTIVE NONEVALUATIVE SPECIFIC NOT GLOBAL

Get the group to write their own examples and check these.
4. Preparing action plans
OH11 Go through the five headings using the overhead giving examples from handout No. 9 plus others of your own as necessary.

GOOD ACTION PLANS SHOULD BE:
MEASURABLE SPECIFIC OUTPUT-ORIENTED
REALISTIC TIME BOUNDED

Get the group to prepare some example action-plan statements and review these.

12.00 LUNCH (ONE HOUR)

1.00 VIDEO MODEL AND ROLE PLAYS 1

The first video model should demonstrate an appraisal interview in a fairly straightforward 'good times' situation, between a headteacher and a departmental head.

Get the group to highlight the key stages of the interview and the skills used, as they are watching the tape.

Go back through the key stages to answer any questions and review their work. If you have time, show the tape a second time, stopping it as the stages are recognized.

2.30 ROLE PLAYS

Trainees should individually prepare for a role play of a typical appraisal situation in their school. The situation should not be too difficult to deal with or too complex.

The preparation should include the writing of openers and other key questions, plus details of the appraisee's job, performance and character.

The format for the role plays is:

1. Divide the group into 3s.
2. Each will take turn in being either the appraiser, appraisee or observer. The roles will rotate.
3. Firstly, the appraiser will give some background on the situation to the appraisee.
4. The appraisee should elaborate his or her position as necessary but without becoming too 'clever', difficult or dramatic.
5. Each role play should last, at most, 20 minutes, allowing between 5 and 10 minutes for feedback.
6. The observer should take notes using the observation sheet provided.
7. The observer should give specific, descriptive feedback, starting with positive comments, then asking the appraiser if he or she can identify possible improvements, then giving his or her own ideas for possible improvements.

Two forms of observer guide are included:

- Force-field analysis
- Role-player rating sheet

OPTION: Using closed circuit television to video the role plays. This would greatly increase the time taken but would mean that the observer could illustrate his or her comments by showing scenes from the tape.

3.00 COFFEE (15 minutes)

3.15 VIDEO MODEL AND ROLE PLAYS (continued)

If you have no time beyond 5 p.m. then you will only have time to play the second video sequence, which should show a more difficult appraisal interview. The procedure is as for the first video sequence. You will have no time for a second set of role plays.

If you DO have time, by carrying on after 5 p.m. then a similar procedure should be adopted to the first set of role plays, except this time involving a slightly more difficult case.

5.00 FINISH

DAY 2

9.00 Target setting and appraisal (talk)

A talk to explain the advantages of target setting and appraisal to the individual, to the school and to the LEA.

10.15 COFFEE

10.30 Video model and role plays

This third video should demonstrate an appraisal going wrong between a headteacher and head of department.

Get the group to highlight the 'mistakes' in the interview and then to select the three most fundamental. Debate and agree on the three.

List these three appraisal interview errors.

Aim to avoid those three in the role plays ahead.

Divide group into 3s, and operate as before, this time using cases prepared by the trainer as handouts. Two case studies are included: Case Study No. 1 TOM BRAGSBY; and Case Study No. 2 JOHN SCRAWN.

12.15 LUNCH

1.30 Role plays using CCTV (continued)

3.00 COFFEE

3.15 Following the interview.

1. Writing up a report of the interview. Ask the group 'Why do we need to write up the appraisal? Summarize their answers on a flip, ensuring the key points are brought out. Consolidate with handout No. 10.

2. Following up the action plan. Explain that appraisal cannot help to improve performance if nothing is done about the plans afterwards. Ask the group 'how can we ensure that good intentions turn into action?' Summarizing their ideas on the flipchart.

3.45 APPRAISAL ADMINISTRATION

Go through the appraisal administration system for your school or LEA.

4.30 WIND UP

Hand out the 'individual action-plan' sheets (handout No. 11). Ask them to fill them in there and then. The plan should focus on those things that the trainees particularly want to do better in future interviews, on improvements they want to make to their appraisal systems, on research they need to do, and so on. They should be examples of good action plans.

Hand out the reaction questionnaires. These should be filled in immediately and collected for the trainer to analyze (handout No. 12).

5.00 CLOSE THE COURSE.

APPRAISAL INTERVIEWING: FORCE-FIELD ANALYSIS — OBSERVER'S GUIDE

INSTRUCTIONS

During this appraisal interview two basic kinds of behaviour can be observed:

1. Behaviour that helps the progress of the interview, e.g., reaching agreement, resolving differences, clarifying issues, developing a course of action, asking questions, clarifying purpose, avoiding win-lose behaviour.
2. Behaviour that hinders the progress of the interview, e.g., interruption, blocking out, disagreement, failure to listen or explore, taking a dogmatic position.

Note any examples of the first kind of behaviour (helping behaviour) in the first column on the force-field format chart. Then note examples of hindering behaviour in the second column. After the role play is complete, consider your replies to the questions at the foot of the sheet. Be prepared to discuss your observations and recommendations with the group.

FORCE FIELD FORMAT

Examples of helping behaviour	Examples of hindering behaviour
1.	1.
2.	2.
3.	3.
4.	4.

1. What could be done to reduce hindering behaviour?
2. What could be done to increase helping behaviour?
3. Other comments:

ROLE PLAYER RATING SHEET

DIRECTIONS

1. There is no 'good' or 'bad' end on the first nine scales A–I. Whether one should be flexible or firm, etc., depends on the situation.
2. On each of the nine scales A–I circle the number that represents your opinion of what the role player did.
3. Underline the number that represents your opinion of what should have been done.
4. The difference between the circled and the underlined number represents the 'error' of that factor in that situation.
5. Circle one number of the overall rating to indicate your general reaction to the role player's effectiveness.

Role Player: Observer:
Situation:

Date:

					(Difference)
A.	General approach	Flexible	1 2 3 4 5 6 7	Firm	( )
B.	Who was in control?	Leader	1 2 3 4 5 6 7	Subordinate	( )
C.	Communication by appraiser	Talk	1 2 3 4 5 6 7	Listen	( )
D.	Attitude	Tense	1 2 3 4 5 6 7	Relaxed	( )
E.	Approach	Person	1 2 3 4 5 6 7	Problem	( )
F.	Relationship from appraiser to appraisee	Friendly	1 2 3 4 5 6 7	Cold	( )
G.	Tone	Formal	1 2 3 4 5 6 7	Informal	( )
H.	Style of appraiser	Directive	1 2 3 4 5 6 7	Nondirective	( )
I.	Speed	Rapid	1 2 3 4 5 6 7	Slow	( )
			OVERALL RATING		
		Poor	1 2 3 4 5 6 7	Good	

Comment by observer:

APPRAISAL HANDOUT NO. 1

PREPARING FOR AN APPRAISAL INTERVIEW

At the appraisal interview, perhaps more than any other time, the appraiser is under review. Under review to see if you can be bothered as an individual and as a senior representative of the SCHOOL, to consider it important enough to take time to prepare. Also you are under review to face the facts.

One thing is very clear, though, and this is that any lack of preparation registers as disinterest to the TEACHER.

Preparation also affects your ability to make a success of the interview. Without the right data, feedback or planning will be generalized and incomplete. The following list below will help you to prepare:

1. Fix mutually convenient time.
2. Do not fill the whole day with appraisal interviews.
3. Describe to the TEACHER in advance, the reasons for the meeting and the procedure.
4. If possible give the TEACHER a preparation document or a list of key questions to think about.
5. Read and review relevant sources of data such as job descriptions, objectives, comments received, last year's appraisal and future plans.
6. Make a note of any key points you wish to make or questions you would like to ask.
7. Prepare the interview room.
8. Ensure there will be no interruptions.

Handout No. 2 will help you to think over and analyze the key issues which you hope to address at the interview.

APPRAISAL HANDOUT NO. 2

FACTORS INFLUENCING PERFORMANCE

APTITUDE Aptitude is potential to do something, e.g. intelligence or artistic flair. Aptitudes, it must be assumed, cannot be changed. Multiplied by:

LEARNING Learning includes knowledge and skills gained through experience or training. Equals:

ABILITY Capacity to do the job, i.e., the necessary basic qualities and potential and the required knowledge and skills. This multiplied by:

MOTIVATION Willingness to do the job, based upon the employee's own needs and his or her perception of the records available as a result of work. Equals:

PERFORMANCE Performance here relates to productivity/the achievement of objectives and standards. Multiplied by:

ATTITUDE Predisposition to think, feel or act in a certain way, based on past experiences. Altogether equals:

OVERALL CONTRIBUTION The value of an employee to the school as a whole. There are in addition, other external factors which influence the performance achieved by an individual against objectives and standards:

TECHNOLOGY The equipment and work methods used.
ORGANIZATION The way responsibilities and authority are distributed.
OBJECTIVES AND STANDARDS The quality of the objectives and standards set and their reasonableness. Also the extent to which priorities change.

APPRAISAL HANDOUT NO. 3

FOUR BASIC FORMS OF PERFORMANCE DISCUSSION

Heads talk to the staff of the school about many different work-related subjects. Each of these discussions about work assumes one of four basic forms, directly related to its purpose:

1. Discovery
2. Problem solving
3. Announcement/direction
4. Persuasion/negotiation

To communicate well as a HEAD, it is important to be able to lead all four of these basic forms of discussion, and to know which is most appropriate for a particular situation.

The DISCOVERY form of work discussion is to be used in all situations where one's immediate purpose is to get information. When a HEAD interviews a person to determine whether or not to hire him or her, or when a HEAD is hearing a complaint or wants to solicit a TEACHER'S ideas about a plan, the discovery form is the right one (M4/S4 Delegation).

The PROBLEM-SOLVING form of work discussion is used when the HEAD wants to assist others in finding and trying out new ways of doing things. This form is the right one for talking to TEACHERS about developing new and better ways to do their work or for helping them to solve personal problems that are negatively affecting their work (M3/S4 Participation).

The ANNOUNCEMENT/DIRECTION form of work discussion should be used when a HEAD wants to tell a TEACHER about new policies, changes in the timetable, or any change which has already been decided upon (M1/S1 Tell).

The PERSUASION/NEGOTIATION form of work discussion is used when the purpose of the discussion is to 'sell' an idea. This form is appropriate in public relations, or in pushing recommendations for changes which have to compete with other recommendations or with just plain inertia (M2/S2 Sell).

APPRAISAL HANDOUT NO. 4

THE BASIC STRUCTURE OF ALL WORK DISCUSSIONS

BASIC STRUCTURE	GOAL	USUAL TIME SPENT
Climate	To establish a relaxed and open mood; to get other person to feel ready to offer ideas and opinions	1–2 minutes
Openers	To focus the attention of the person; to get right to the heart of the matter	45–60 seconds
Exploration	(a) To get other person to show what he/she knows	3 minutes or more
	(b) To consider very important elements of the subject the other person might overlook	20 minutes or more Usually 70–80% of the time for the whole discussion
Closure	To summarize To make sure the 'next step' is clear to the other person. To increase likelihood of follow through.	1–5 minutes

APPRAISAL HANDOUT NO. 5

OUTLINE FOR THE APPRAISAL INTERVIEW

CLIMATE: Relaxed; receptive; private
OPENERS: Theme Line/s — state the purpose of the overall appraisal interview or main stage of the interview.

Cue Line — an open-ended question that gets the TEACHER talking on the subject in question.

EXPLORATION:

1. PERFORMANCE REVIEW

Review the objectives or standards set for the past year and agree upon the extent to which they have been achieved.

2. PERFORMANCE ANALYSIS

Examine the reasons for achievements or underachievements. See 'Factors

Influencing Performance.' Also look at unavoidable external factors. Agree on the TEACHER'S strengths and weaknesses.

3. INDIVIDUAL NEEDS AND ASPIRATIONS

Short term — discuss ways in which job responsibilities or methods could be adapted to better suit the TEACHER'S needs.

Longer term — discuss the TEACHER'S career goals. Review the likely opportunities for the goals to be achieved. Examine the extent to which the TEACHER'S skills and knowledge match up to the career moves in question.

4. FUTURE JOB REQUIREMENTS

Discuss changes in job responsibilities or methods already planned and projects/objectives/targets for the coming year.

CLOSURE: Agree and summarize a plan to achieve improved performance and, where appropriate, development of the TEACHER over the coming year.

AIR TIME: 70/30 (70% TEACHER/30% HEAD)

HELPFUL HINTS: Adopt a problem-solving style. Encourage the employee to take the initiative on solutions. Utilize open-ended questions, listening techniques and make feedback descriptive and specific.

APPRAISAL HANDOUT NO. 6

THE STRUCTURE AND FUNCTION OF WORK-DISCUSSION OPENERS

	PURPOSE	HELPFUL HINTS	TIME
THEME LINE/S (usually not more than 4 sentences)	To identify the purpose of the work discussion. Briefly to set the limits of its concern.	Set it up as results desired from the discussion	30–40 secs
CUE LINE	To get the other person to start talking. To get the other person to respond directly to the subject of	Start sentence with the words *what* or *how*	5 secs

the theme line/s.
To get a positive
and helpful
response to the
subject of the
'theme' line/s

It may be helpful to think of the 'openers' in this way:

The theme line/s create a space to be explored — they identify a particular room with a set of walls.

The cue line shows the person being interviewed where the door is for entering the space set out in the theme line/s.

Theme lines create the room.

Cue lines show where the entry is for the person being interviewed.

Appraisal interview openers

Theme Line/s should state the purpose of the overall appraisal interview or main stage of the interview.

Cue line should be an open-ended question, i.e., a question that cannot be answered with Yes or No and gets the TEACHER talking on the subject in question.

Illustrations

Theme Line: 'One of the main aims of this interview is to look at your performance over the past year. As you can see, we both have copies of your objectives.'

Cue Line: 'What progress did you make with objective number one?'

Theme Line: 'Before we make definite plans for changing your responsibilities for next year we need to consider your own development and personal aim within education.'

Cue Line: 'What thoughts do you have on where you would like to be in, say, two years from now?'

APPRAISAL HANDOUT NO. 7

LISTENING SKILLS

SILENCE with nonverbal signs of listening such as eye contact and facial expression.

ACKNOWLEDGEMENTS — verbal and active nonverbal signs of attention (nodding your head, 'Uh-huh,' 'I see')

DOOR OPENERS/PRODS — words that invite the other person to talk or carry on talking ('Would you like to talk about that?' 'Please go on')
PARAPHRASING — summarizing or rephrasing what the other person has said in your own words.
REFLECTING FEELINGS — feeding back to the sender what you perceive to be his or her feelings ('You seem angry about that', 'You are obviously delighted')

Benefits from using listening skills

- You give the other person a chance to express himself or herself, to get things, 'off his or her chest'.
- You demonstrate to the other person that you have heard, understood and accurately interpreted what he or she said.
- The other person is encouraged toward being his or her own problem solver.

APPRAISAL HANDOUT NO. 8

GIVING FEEDBACK

Feedback, to be effective, needs to be:

- Descriptive rather than evaluative

'Last term you missed the deadline for handing in pupil reports on three occasions' is descriptive.
'You are obviously incapable of getting things done on time' is evaluative.

- Specific rather than global

'Your GCE passes were 55% up upon last year' is specific.
'Examination results are pretty good' is global.

Specific, descriptive feedback is likely to lead to problem-solving behaviour. Global, evaluative feedback is likely to lead to defensiveness.

EXERCISE

Read the following examples of feedback. Put a D at the end of each example you feel is descriptive, S if specific, E if evaluative, and G if global:

'When you told the CEO to call back when you were less busy you probably affected your promotion prospects.'

'Somehow I just don't feel you're pulling your weight.'

'On a scale of 1 to 10 I'd put your level of initiative at 7.'

'I noticed you welcoming that visitor to the school. You were courteous and helpful and the visitor was obviously pleased.'

'I'm proud to have you on my staff. That's all I need to say.'

'Well, on my count you've only managed to type seven letters today.'

Write below an example of specific, descriptive feedback concerning a situation you have experienced recently:

APPRAISAL HANDOUT NO. 9

PREPARING ACTION PLANS

Good action plans should be:

- Measurable

'Increase the percentage of parents attending school reporting evenings' *not*

'Improve parental support of the school'.

- Specific

'Make 200 new flashcards by the end of term' *not*

'Make a significant increase in the stock of flashcards in the department.'

- Realistic/attainable

Motivation to do something is to a large extent determined by the expectation we have of succeeding.

Overambitious objectives can lead to frustration and disillusionment.

- Time bonded

'Implement the new computer system by 31 March' *not*

'Get the system in as soon as possible.'

APPRAISAL HANDOUT NO. 10

WRITING A REPORT OF THE INTERVIEW

Under 'Preparation' one of the items suggested for you to review in advance was last year's appraisal report on the teacher. This is not the only reason for writing a report on the interview. Reports will probably be placed on personal files, they will, it is hoped, be used as the basis of a personal reference, for future training needs in the school and so on. Also the report is a valuable *aide-mémoire* for agreed plans. It may be useful if an internal up-grading is being considered.

So how do you fill in the appraisal forms? During the interview you probably have jotted down some notes. After the interview you should get down to completing the form immediately.

The report should be an accurate summary of the meeting and include no new significant data. Remember that good feedback should be specific and descriptive.

If you do not already have an appraisal scheme you could use any free time on this course to begin to design one. Each school may have a slightly different emphasis it wants to place on different aspects of appraisal, and administration will almost certainly vary from school to school or even within a single school.

APPRAISAL HANDOUT NO. 11

INDIVIDUAL ACTION PLAN

Date:

List below the ideas from this course which seem to you to be worth introducing in your school. Where possible prepare an outline plan to bring about the introduction.

Concepts of ideas to introduced	*Outline plan to bring about the introduction*

APPRAISAL HANDOUT NO. 12

REACTION QUESTIONNAIRE

Course: Course leader:
Date: Position:
Name:

Please circle the numbers that best represent your reactions to each subject.

Course content

Totally Irrelevant	1 2 3 4 5 6 7 8 9 10	Very Relevant

Course methods

Totally Ineffective	1 2 3 4 5 6 7 8 9 10	Very Effective

Course leader		
Poor	1 2 3 4 5 6 7 8 9 10	Excellent
Overall effectiveness		
Doubtful Value	1 2 3 4 5 6 7 8 9 10	Very Effective

Comments:

EQUIPMENT AND MATERIALS

Flipchart and pens
Overhead projector and screen
11 overhead slides
3 modelling sequences on video cassette
1 participant handout per trainee
2 observation sheets per trainee
1 reaction questionnaire per trainee
1 individual plan-for-action form per trainee

IF CLOSED CIRCUIT TV IS USED

1 or more black-and-white or colour video camera with tripod
1 or more video-cassette recorder or video reel-to-reel recorder with black-and-white or colour monitor
1 or more microphones with stand (if not incorporated in camera)
1 or more blank video cassettes or video reel-to-reel tapes

REFERENCES

Anthony, R. N. and Herzlinger, R. E. (1980) *Management Control in Nonprofit Organizations*, Irwin Dorsey Limited, Ontario

Bernstein, D. (1983) *Working for Customers*, Confederation of British Industry, London

Blanchard, K. and Johnson, S. (1983a) *The One Minute Manager*, Willow Books, London

Blanchard, K. and Johnson, S. (1983b) *Putting the One Minute Manager to Work*, Willow Books, London

Britton, J. (1969) *Talking to learn*. In D. Barnes et al. (1969) Language, The Learner And The School, Penguin Books, Harmondsworth

Brown, M. and others (1985) *No Turning Back: a new agenda from a group of Conservative MPs*, Conservative Political Centre, Crawley

Bunnell, S. and Stephens, E. (1984) *Teacher Appraisal: a democratic approach, school organisation 4.4*, CSCS, York

Cave, R. and Cave, J. (1985) *Teacher Appraisal and Promotion*, R. & J. Cave, Education Consultants, Norwich

Committee of Heads of Educational Institutions (1986) *Performance Appraisal of Heads and Principals*, National Association of Headteachers, Haywards Heath

Department of Education and Science (1985a) *Better Schools: a summary*, HMSO, London

Department of Education and Science (1985b) *Quality in Schools: evaluation and appraisal*, HMSO, London

Drucker, P. (1955) *The Practice of Management*, Heinemann, London

Everard, K. B. and Morris, G. (1984) *Effective School Management*, Harper and Row, London

Granger, C. H. (1964) The hierarchy of objectives, *Harvard Business Review*, May/June, Vol. 43, No. 3, pp. 63–74

Hancock, D. (1985) Staff appraisal in schools and colleges — a view from D.E.S. A talk by the Permanent Secretary, Department of Education and Science, to Education for Industrial Society Conference, 25 February

Hersey, P. and Blanchard, K. (1982) *Management of Organizational Behaviour: utilizing human resources*, Prentice-Hall Inc., Englewood Cliffs, NJ

Herzberg, F. (1966) *Work and the Nature of Man*, World Publishing, New York

Lyn Jones, J. (1983) Hillingdon LEA: the future place of curriculum review: teacher appraisal within schools, *Evaluation in Education*, November, No. 6

McKenzie, I. (1986) Teacher appraisal: problems and practicalities, AMMA

Education Conference report, London
Maier, N. R. (1976) *The Appraisal Interview: three basic approaches*, University Associates, La Jolla CA
Margarison, C. (1976) Turning the annual appraisal system upside down, *Industrial Training International*, February
Maslow, A. H. (1954) *Motivation and Personality*, Harper and Row, New York
Morgan, C., Hall, V. and Mackay, H. (1983) *The Selection of Secondary School Headteachers,* Open University Press, Milton Keynes
Murphy, J. (1984) School climate and factors which influence it, *Rostrum*, Autumn, APVC, Dublin
Packwood, T. (1977) The school as a hierarchy, *Educational Administration*, Vol. 5, No. 2
Peter, L. J. and Hull, R. (1969) *The Peter Principle: why things always go wrong*, Souvenir, London
Peters, T. and Austin, N. (1985) *A Passion for Excellence*, Guild Publishing, London
Peters, T. J. and Waterman, R. H. (1982) *In Search of Excellence*, Harper and Row, New York
Phillips, K. and Fraser, T. (1982) *The Management of Interpersonal Skills Training*, Gower, Aldershot
Randell, G., Shaw, R., Packard, P. and Slater, J. (1972) *Staff Appraisal*, Institute of Personnel Management, London
Stewart, A. and Stewart, V. (1977) *Practical Performance Appraisal*, Gower, Aldershot
Stewart, R. (1963) *The Reality of Management*, Pan Books, London
Stewart, V. and Stewart, A. (1982) *Managing the Poor Performer*, Gower, Aldershot
Suffolk Education Department (1985) *Those Having Torches: teacher appraisal: a study funded by the DES*, Ipswich
Thomson, A. and Thomson, L. (1984) *What Learning Looks Like*, Longmans for Schools Council, London
Trethowan, D. M. (1981) The missing link, managing the head, *The Head*, Vol. 1, No. 5, November
Trethowan, D. M. (1983a) *Delegation*, Education for Industrial Society, London
Trethowan, D. M. (1983b) *Target Setting*, Education for Industrial Society, London
Trethowan, D. M. (1984) *The Leadership of Schools*, Education for Industrial Society, London
Trethowan, D. M. (1985a) *Communication in Schools*, Education for Industrial Society, London
Trethowan, D. M. (1985b) *Industrial means to educational ends*, in Contributions No. 8, Summer, CSCS, York
Trethowan, D. M. (1985c) *Teamwork in Schools*, Education for Industrial Society, London
Trethowan, D. M. and Smith, D. L. (1984) *Induction,* Education for Industrial Society, London
Warwick, D. (1983) *Staff Appraisal*, Education for Industrial Society, London

INDEX